# HOW TO MINISTER TO FAMILIES IN YOUR CHURCH

## Phillip H. Waugh

LifeWay Press
Nashville, Tennessee

**ISBN 0-6330-2900-9**

Dewey Decimal Classification: 259.1
Subject Headings: CHURCH WORK WITH FAMILIES \ FAMILY MINISTRY

This book is the text for course LS-0034 in the Christian Growth Study Plan.

Scripture quotations marked NIV are from the Holy Bible,
*New International Version,* copyright © 1973, 1978, 1984
by International Bible Society.

Scripture quotations marked NKJV are from the *New King James Version.*
Copyright © 1982, Thomas Nelson, Inc., Publishers. Used by permission.

Scripture quotations marked NASB are from the *New American Standard Bible,*
© Copyright The Lockman Foundation, 1960, 1962, 1963, 1968, 1971, 1972, 1973,
1975, 1977, 1995. Used by permission.

The author wishes to express special appreciation to John Franklin for his contribution to the
section "God Speaks Through Prayer" in chapter 1, to Richard Leach for his contribution to the
section "Outreach" in chapter 2, and to Linda Ranson-Pallemino for her contribution to the
section "Single-Parent Family Ministry" in chapter 8. The author would also like to thank
the state family-ministry directors who contribute to the development and distribution of
this resource. Without the involvement of state directors, family ministry on the Convention,
state, associational, and church levels would be greatly hindered.

Order additional copies of this book by writing to LifeWay Church Resources Customer Service,
MSN 113; 127 Ninth Avenue, North; Nashville, TN 37234-0013; by calling toll free
(800) 458-2772; by faxing (615) 251-5933; by ordering online at *www.lifeway.com;*
by emailing *customerservice@lifeway.com;* or by visiting a LifeWay Christian Store.

For information about adult discipleship and family resources, training, and events,
visit our Web site at *www.lifeway.com/discipleplus.*

*Printed in the United States of America*

LifeWay Press
127 Ninth Avenue, North
Nashville, TN 37234-0151

As God works through us, we will help people and churches know Jesus Christ and seek
His kingdom by providing biblical solutions that spiritually transform individuals and cultures.

# Contents

# Preface

The fact that you are reading this book indicates that God wants you to consider joining Him in ministering to families in your church and community. I firmly believe that God is working all around us and that He has placed this resource in your hand. God may have used a minister in your church or a fellow Christian to ask you to consider working with families. He may have used circumstances in your family life or in the lives of families around you to plant the desire in your heart to minister to families. Whatever the method and for whatever the reason, God is the One who raises the concern or creates the desire for us to do kingdom work, and that is what this resource is all about.

As you study this resource, I encourage you to pray for God's desire for your life and your church. The need to minister to the families around the world has never been greater. The church in our culture and in other cultures as well claims to value the family and its importance to the kingdom of God while failing to provide appropriate and adequate ministries to support these claims. The church needs to respond with conviction that God desires to use the family to provide a witness of His love to the world.

In this book I share with you my beliefs and my desires for you and family ministry. As you consider family ministry, you must begin with self-examination. What you believe about God determines what you believe about marriage and family. These beliefs shape your ministry to couples, parents, and their children. Your theology—your beliefs about God and His activity in the world—directly affects the way you view others and relate to them. As Henry Blackaby stated in *Experiencing God: Knowing and Doing the Will of God*, "What we do reveals what we really believe."[1]

Do you believe that God is real? Do you believe that He is actively involved in His creation? Do you believe that He is always at work around you, pursuing a continual love relationship with you? I believe that God is real and that He pursues a love relationship with me that is real and personal. I believe that He has established the family as an arena of human relationships through which He expresses His love for me in ways and to degrees unlike any other arena of human relationships.

Join me as we examine God's intention for the family and learn ways we can be a part of His ministry to families in our churches and communities. My goal is for this book to inspire you and equip you to minister to families in your church and community no matter what the size of your congregation may be. God is raising up individuals in His church to join Him in ministering to families across North America and around the world. Will you join Him in this ministry?

---

[1]Henry T. Blackaby and Claude V. King, *Experiencing God: Knowing and Doing the Will of God* (Nashville: LifeWay, 1990), 111.

# The Heart of Family Ministry

The heart of family ministry, like any ministry of the church, should come from the heart of God. Its focus should be not on what we can do for families and how we can enrich families but on what God wants for families and how we can join Him in what He is doing for them. We should ask ourselves: *What is God saying to us about ministering to the needs of families? How are we responding to His invitation to join Him in meeting those needs? How are we applying His teachings to various family stages, situations, systems, structures, and settings in our church?* When we seek answers to those questions, we find that God's heart—His desire—is to build strong families. How do we accomplish this? Where do we begin? How do we achieve our goal, and how do we measure our success?

At a conference for Christian counselors in Dallas, one of the presenters, a well-known author in the area of marriage, was making a presentation on developing a ministry to married couples. During his presentation he introduced a particular point by saying, "Now let me share three easy steps for you to take in developing a successful mentoring ministry." Everyone immediately began searching for a pencil and paper to jot down these three steps. Then the presenter said: "I must confess that I have tricked you. You see, there are no easy steps for developing this ministry. You have to find your own pathway to a successful ministry that is right for you and your church." I silently applauded a kindred spirit in ministry.

Too often we get caught up in the three easy steps or 10 tasks for achieving a goal and fail to acknowledge the uniqueness of the ministry God has given to us and us alone. While providing information, insight, and inspiration, this book does not seek to provide the one way to minister to families in your church. Any resource that seeks to do this fails to understand the uniqueness of God's creation. Because each church is unique, each must seek the path of ministry to which God is directing us, following His directions as we go. If we all walked the same path of ministry day in and day out, we would soon find ourselves in a rut.

Family ministry is not a church program. Ministry to families, as one of the basic functions of the church, is a core value that is to be emphasized in all aspects of church life. Ministering to the needs of families must be purpose-driven, not program-driven. All family activities, studies, events, resources, and ministries need to serve a purpose. They need to focus on meeting a particular need in the families of the church and/or community. The reason to provide these ministries is for families to experience the love of God through His church.

> **Ministering to the needs of families must be purpose-driven**

This chapter illustrates how you can join God in ministering to the families around you. God speaks to us by the Holy Spirit in various ways. He speaks to us "through the Bible, prayer, circumstances, and the church to reveal Himself, His purposes, and His ways."[1] Each of these avenues is equally important in discovering how God is working to meet the needs of families.

## God Speaks Through the Bible

One avenue through which God speaks to us is the Bible. Therefore, as we begin a ministry to families, we need to explore what God is saying to us through His Word. Although the Bible does not define *family* for us, it is clear that a family in the Bible is a group of persons related to one another by marriage and birth or adoption. However, the structure of the traditional or nuclear family as we understand it today was not common during biblical times. In fact, those who gather for family reunions today would have been considered the traditional family of old. Although the structure of the family has changed somewhat, the biblical concept of family has not changed. What can we discover about God's heart for families through His Word?

*The family is established and ordained by God.* The Book of Genesis records that God created the family and blessed it. In Genesis 1:26 God said He would create man in His image to rule over creation. In verse 27 He created man and woman. In verse 28 He blessed them and then pronounced His creation as very good in Genesis 1:31.

When Genesis 1:28 says that God blessed Adam and Eve, it means that God gave His approval to an action and empowered them to complete the action successfully.[2] When God blesses a union between man and woman, it is holy because God is holy and because He empowers the couple to complete the marriage successfully. Apart from God, man and woman cannot successfully accomplish that which He created them to accomplish in their union. Without Him they cannot know the

**God created the family and blessed it**

intimate relationship He intends. They cannot " 'be fruitful and multiply; fill the earth and subdue it; have dominion over … every living thing that moves on the earth' " (v. 28, NKJV).

In Genesis 2:18-25 we learn several things about the way God views marriage and family. First we see in verse 18 that marriage was initiated to provide companionship and to dispel loneliness. We also see that God provided someone to be Adam's suitable helper to walk alongside him. Look at Adam's response to the woman in verse 23. He didn't just name her like the animals in the garden. He immediately recognized that she was bone of his bones and flesh of his flesh. Then in verse 25 we see a righteous couple, and we are introduced to what I believe is God's definition of *intimacy*: "The man and his wife were both naked, and they felt no shame" (NIV). When a husband and wife can stand naked physically, mentally, emotionally, and spiritually before God and not be ashamed, they are standing on holy ground and are experiencing the ultimate intimate relationship between two persons. That experience, which is reserved for the married couple, reveals the depth of intimacy God desires with us.

*God desires to bless all families of the earth.* God's words to Abram in Genesis 12:1-3 reveal this truth.

> Now the Lord had said to Abram:
> "Get out of your country,
> From your family
> And from your father's house,
> To a land that I will show you.
> I will make you a great nation;
> I will bless you
> And make your name great;
> And you shall be a blessing.
> I will bless those who bless you,
> And I will curse him who curses you;
> And in you all the families of the earth shall be blessed" (NKJV).

Do you recall what God did in Genesis 1:28? He blessed the man and the woman. Do you recall what God's blessing means? He gives His approval to an action and empowers someone to complete the action successfully. In Genesis 12:1-3 God blessed all families through the family of one man who responded in obedience to Him. "All" families include your family and the families in your church and community.

*God views family from an eternal perspective.* In the beginning God was. He existed before time began. From the beginning of time He has viewed family from an eternal perspective. He told Jeremiah,

> "Before I formed you in the womb I knew you;
> Before you were born I sanctified you;
> I ordained you a prophet to the nations" (Jer. 1:5, NKJV)

The psalmist declared in Psalm 139:14-16:

> I will praise You, for I am fearfully and wonderfully made;
> Marvelous are your works,
> And that my soul knows very well.
> My frame was not hidden from You,
> When I was made in secret,
> And skillfully wrought in the lowest parts of the earth.
> Your eyes saw my substance, being yet unformed.
> And in Your book they all were written,
> The days fashioned for me,
> When as yet there were none of them (NKJV).

Just as God, who is eternal, knows us as individuals before we were formed in our mother's womb and knows the days He has fashioned, He also knows when a family is being born as well, even before it is formed. And as families are born, God is at work, not just in and for that individual family or for that particular generation but for generations to come. God's plan for family extends beyond the immediate to the eternal. He views families from generation to generation, and He is the only One who can complete the blessing successfully.

> **God's plan for family extends beyond the immediate to the eternal**

*God established the family as the first arena of human relationships, through which He pursues a continuing love relationship with us as individuals.* Family relationships should model and witness to the love relationship between Christ and the church. Ephesians 5:21-33 sets forth the way families should model the relationship between Christ and His bride, the church. It also sets forth the way we as the family of God are to relate to Him as the head or husband and father of the family. This passage has important implications for matters of submission, unconditional love, sanctification, holiness, and servanthood. Remember the blessing in Genesis? God does not require of us anything He has not first blessed us to keep. I believe that God has chosen to love me through my wife. He demonstrates His unconditional love for me through her. He allows me to perfect holiness in matrimony as I learn to receive and demonstrate unconditional love in marriage. Love, as depicted in Romans 12:9-13, is "without hypocrisy." Love abhors what is evil and clings to what is good; is "kindly affectionate to one another, … in honor giving preference to one another." Love is not lazy or proud; it is "fervent in spirit, serving the Lord; rejoicing in hope, patient in tribulation, continuing steadfastly in prayer; distributing to the needs of the saints, given to hospitality" (NKJV). These verses teach husbands and wives how to express their love for each other and for God. A love that calls us to totally submit to Him and to willingly lay down our lives for another is a love after God's own heart.

*God uses the family to teach what He has done for His people and to identify work He wants to do.* In Exodus 13:8-16, in the context of family, Moses was instructed to establish certain religious observances so that " 'when your son asks you in time to come, saying, "What is this?" that you shall say to him, "By strength of hand the Lord brought us out of Egypt, out of the house of bondage" ' " (v. 14, NKJV). And in Joshua 4:6-7,21-24 we read that God provided passage for His people through the Jordan River. The leaders of the 12 tribes were instructed to take stones from the riverbed and place them on the bank of the Jordan. When asked why they were to do this, Joshua responded, " 'that this may be a sign among you when your children ask in time to come, saying, "What do these stones mean to you?" Then you shall answer them that the waters of the Jordan were cut off before the ark of the covenant of the Lord; when it crossed over the Jordan' " (vv. 6-7, NKJV). The families were to teach the generations to come what God had done in the past in order to authenticate His activity in the present.

*The family is the basic arena through which we are to serve, evangelize, and minister with one another and to others.* You will find in Acts 16:14-15 the account of Lydia, who heard the gospel from Paul: "The Lord opened her heart to heed the things spoken by Paul. And when she and her household were baptized, she begged us, saying, 'If you have judged me to be faithful to the Lord, come to my house and stay' " (NKJV). In verses 30-31 is the account of the jailer who, in fear or despair, was about to take his own life when Paul called to him and verified that the prisoners had not escaped. "He brought them out and said, 'Sirs, what must I do to be saved?' So they said, 'Believe on the Lord Jesus Christ, and you will be saved, you and your household' " (NKJV). Scripture affirms that the family is the best arena of human relationships in and through which we are introduced and introduce others to the gospel of Jesus Christ (see Acts 18:26-27; Rom. 16:3; 1 Cor. 7:12-17; 16:17-19).

No matter how great our love is for our family, the family is not to come before our relationship with God or to replace our devotion to Him. First Corinthians 7:25-40 admonishes us not to place family relationships over our relationship with the Lord.

*The family is usually the first to bear the brunt of our sin against God and is most affected by our sin.* Although the family can become a spawning ground for sin, it can learn of God's work through mistakes, crises, and grief processes. In Genesis 4 when Cain became angry with God, he lashed out at Abel, who became the victim of Cain's sin against God. In Genesis 42—46 when Jacob showed favoritism toward Joseph, it set in motion a chain of events in Joseph's life, beginning with his brothers' plot to kill him. In 2 Samuel 13—20 we see in the account of Absalom, Amnon, and Tamar the way sin tore that family apart. But we can also read of the way God worked through their mistakes, crises, and grief to bring healing and restoration to Him.

*The church, as the family of God, should support and care for one another.* The church is not to replace the family but to join God in ministering to the family and to expand the concept of family through enhancing, educating, strengthening, guiding, and loving the family. Romans 12:15 says, "Rejoice with those who rejoice, and weep with those who weep" (NKJV). As a church we have an opportunity to do this with families. We can join God in the lives of these families, coming alongside them and offering them comfort and hope. We are admonished in Galatians 6:2 to "bear one another's burdens, and so fulfill the law of Christ" (NKJV). When a family joins our church, we should view it as an activity of God in which He affords us an opportunity to demonstrate our love for Him by loving these families, demonstrating for them what it means to be the family of God.

> The church is to join God in ministering to the family

## God Speaks Through Prayer

Not only does God speak to us by the Holy Spirit through His Word, but He also speaks through prayer. We need to pray for God's heart in ministering to families. Every segment of society today finds itself assaulted by forces that threaten to destroy it. Nowhere is this truer than the family, in which the divorce rate, the illegitimacy rate, domestic abuse, parental relations with teens and children, and a host of other evils continue to worsen. Such realities no longer surprise anyone, but most people seem confused about where to turn to solve the problem.

The beginning point remains the same as it has been for generations—prayer. In the Bible whenever any situation changed, intense, fervent prayer preceded it. When David was being pursued by Saul, he prayed, and God delivered him. When the Assyrians invaded Israel, Hezekiah prayed, and God delivered the nation. When Herod imprisoned Peter, the church prayed, and God set him free. The scriptural pattern indicates that prayer precedes God's work on our behalf; therefore, we can safely assume that fervent prayer must be made for families in order to see God work supernaturally.

## Praying to Know God's Heart for Family Ministry

For our prayers to be effective, we must ask according to God's will. Avery Willis wrote: "God delights in answering prayer that is asked according to His will, but He refuses to answer prayer that is not consistent with what He wants. We need to hear God's voice so that we will know what to pray."[3] So our primary order of business is to ask God to reveal His will to us about family ministry. Here are practical steps for doing so.

> **Prayer is the act of entering the presence of Holy God**

*Enter His presence with thanksgiving.* Follow the format of the psalmist:

> Enter his gates with thanksgiving
> and his courts with praise;
> give thanks to him and praise his name (Ps. 100:4, NIV).

Prayer is the act of entering the presence of Holy God. As we enter His presence, we are compelled to give thanks.

T. W. Hunt described in *Disciple's Prayer Life* how he became aware of his need for an expanded attitude of thanksgiving:

> I was squeezing my toothpaste onto the toothbrush one morning when I realized that I had never thanked the Lord for toothpaste … I had never thanked Him for my teeth. I wondered: What if tomorrow everything I received depended on my acknowledging its being from God today? If I did not thank God for air and lungs today, there would be no air tomorrow, and my lungs would collapse. Few of us realize how totally dependent on God we are. We do not acknowledge God as the source of everything we have.[4]

What are some things for which you are thankful—resources, tools, ministries, or individuals God has given to your church? Can you name some positive things that are happening in your church? What about some positive things that are happening in the families in your church? What are some of the provisions God has made for your church? Stop and give thanks to God for what He is doing in your family and church.

*Enter His courts with praise.* The next step in praying for God's heart in family ministry is to praise God for who He is and what He means to your life and to the life of your church. Praise focuses on the person of God. It creates a sense of awe and dependence on God. One way to focus on God's character is through His names. Secure a list of names of God or read Psalm 91 and praise God for who He is and how He has revealed Himself to you and your church.

*Confess sin.* When we pray to know God's heart for family ministry, we also need to confess sin. Read what Isaiah did when he experienced God's glory: " 'Woe to me!' I cried. 'I am ruined! For I am a man of unclean lips, and I live among a people of unclean lips, and my eyes have seen the King, the Lord Almighty' " (Isa. 6:5, NIV). When Isaiah experienced God's glory, he confessed his sin. We need to do the same.

Ask the Lord to search your heart as you read Ephesians 4:22-32. Are there sins you need to confess pertaining to your family, the church, or relationships in the church? Confess those now.

*Present your needs.* Finally, as we seek God's heart for families, we must bring our needs to the throne of grace. In the presence of Holy God, everything is laid bare before Him: "Nothing in all creation is hidden from God's sight. Everything is uncovered and laid bare before the eyes of him to whom we must give account" (Heb. 4:13, NIV). Hebrews 4:14-16 tells us to approach God's throne of grace with confidence—confidence not in yourself or in what you can do for God but in your great High Priest, Jesus, the Son of God. First John 5:14 says, "This is the confidence we have in approaching God: that if we ask anything according to his will, he hears us" (NIV).

### How Can You Pray for Families?

How important is it to pray for families? Of all the things you could pray for, such as salvation, healing, and financial concerns, how does praying for families rank in priority? Based on the preceding Scriptures, we can affirm that family ranks high on God's priority list. God does not view the church through the lens of Sunday School classes, choir, or discipleship groups as much as He views it through the lens of the family. His eternal purposes are carried out through the lifelong institution of the family. Therefore, praying for individuals in the church must include the God-centered element of praying for them in the context of their families.

**Family ranks high on God's priority list**

You can pray for families in two ways. First, pray general prayers of blessing for all families in your church. Two examples are Ephesians 5:22—6:4 and Psalm 78:1-8.

Second, times arise when you can focus your prayers on the particular needs of one family. Answering the questions on the chart below through the Holy Spirit will help you discern God's activity when you pray so that your prayers will be effectual.

# Praying for Families

| Family | Bible | Prayer | Circumstances | Action |
|--------|-------|--------|---------------|--------|
| List names of family members. | What insights and direction are you receiving from Scripture? | What insights and direction are you receiving in prayer? | What doors are opening, challenges are they facing, or discipline are they under? | In light of what God revealed, what action can you take to encourage, assist, or counsel the family? |

Notice the final category on the chart. All of the great prayer warriors of the Bible and history were men and women of boldness and action. Prayer is not the end but the beginning. Prayer puts us in contact with God. When we discern His perspective, we must often respond outwardly by placing our lives alongside those we have prayed for. This means we should always pray with a willingness to become the answer, looking for opportunities to join God by involving our lives in theirs.

When you intercede specifically for a family, what you do in your prayer time is important. Misguided prayer is ineffective prayer. On the other hand, connecting with God and understanding His perspective and purpose for the family create transformational prayer.

## How Can You Lead Your Church to Pray for Families?

The church as a whole is also responsible for praying for families.

1. Educate members on the need to pray for families. Use Scriptures to show them God's perspective on the importance of families. Recognize that this may take time because most people do not readily think in terms of understanding and seeking the ways of God. Education must precede long-term change.

2. Look for existing opportunities for the church to pray for families. Examples:
   - Highlight a family or two in your church bulletin as your prayer focus for the week.
   - Initiate prayer partnerships between existing church families and new families who join the church.
   - Encourage the use of a church-membership list or a pictorial directory as a prayer guide for families.
   - Does your church have an intercessory prayer room? Gather prayer requests from families and compile a list for intercessors to pray for.

   This list is not comprehensive but representative. Ask God to show you opportunities that already exist in your church.

3. Create opportunities for the church to pray for families. The following ideas could be used as special events or as part of a family week.
   - Organize Sunday School class members to pray for the family of another class member.
   - Have a time in the worship service in which societal threats and God's purposes for the family are listed. Lead the congregation in focused prayer time.
   - Model prayer from the pulpit.
   - Hold family prayer meetings in homes in which one family invites another for a meal and prays for them.
   - Encourage family prayer walks during which families pray for other families in the neighborhood.
   - Provide resources on prayer in the family.

   Again, this list is only representative. Ask God to show you specifically what He wants to do through your church.

Think of it: the very God who created the universe, who has all power, for whom nothing is impossible has extended a personal invitation for you to call on Him. Are the challenges facing families in your church too difficult for Him? Could your prayers overtax God's reserves? Will your requests exceed His wisdom? Certainly not! And this very God, your God, delights in answering prayer so that He may show Himself mighty on the behalf of families in your church and community.

> **God has extended a personal invitation for you to call on Him**

## God Speaks Through Circumstances

Another way God speaks to us by the Holy Spirit is through circumstances. By *circumstances* I mean situations in which we find ourselves that may or may not result from the choices we make. If you believe that God is always at work around you, then you must agree that He can and does work through circumstances. The circumstances families face in your church and community vary from household to household. Therefore, you may need to provide families assistance in coping with the present while providing hope for the future.

The word *circumstances* can also refer to what is happening in our culture. The world's view of family, to a great degree, undermines the biblical view of family. For example, *Newsweek* published a special edition on the 21st-century family that stated:

> **The American family does not exist. Rather, we are creating many American families, of diverse styles and shapes. In unprecedented numbers, our families**

are unalike: We have fathers working while mothers keep house; fathers and mothers both working away from the home; single parents; second marriages bringing children together from unrelated backgrounds; childless couples; unmarried couples, with or without children; gay and lesbian [couples and] parents. We are living through a period of historic change in American life.[5]

What is God saying to us through these circumstances? Is He not calling us back to a biblical view of family?

College students, young singles, and many younger married couples are a part of what we call Generation X. Others have labeled this generation 13-teeners because they are the 13th generation in American history. Here are some nationwide characteristics of this generation.

- One out of four was born to a single parent.
- They were the first latchkey kids.
- They are the most racially and ethnically diverse generation in America.
- They are the first generation to have a lower standard of living than their parents.
- One out of three has been physically or sexually abused.
- Half of them have divorced parents.
- They have witnessed more crime than any generation in American history.
- They are the first postindustrial generation.
- They have grown up never knowing trust in national leadership.
- Most sociologists describe this generation as feeling alone.

God has called us to join Him in ministering to the needs of all families in our churches and communities, with the intent of uplifting His ideal of what a family should be. As we look to the immediate future of family ministry, we cannot discount the circumstances that affect any generation of families.

**We must always examine circumstances in light of Scripture**

You must also be ready to join God where He is working in the unexpected circumstances families face. Are the families in your church and community dealing with unemployment, natural disasters, death, new babies, addiction, abuse, an influx of businesses, or unprecedented community growth? All of these circumstances provide opportunities to minister to families.

Is your church receptive to changes brought about by the circumstances families face? God speaks through circumstances, but we must always examine these circumstances in light of Scripture. George Barna states:

Millions of adults express hope that their churches will have a lasting impact on them and their families. In fact, when we asked adults who should be responsible for imparting values to their children, the answers included only three different responses: parents themselves (named by 98 percent), churches (56 percent), and schools (52 percent). Despite these hopes, their disheartening assessment is that churches won't have such an impact. When asked to identify who has the most influence on children's values these days, only 1 percent named churches—ranking them a distant fifth behind friends and peers of their children (33 percent), parents (30 percent), the mass media (21 percent), and schools (13 percent).

Yet if we allow God's influence to permeate our families, real change can result. National Opinion Research Corporation studies have shown that shared prayer can be a powerful means of bonding between husband and wife, leading to a higher probability of a stable and enjoyable marriage. Other studies have indicated that the intensity with which adults accept basic biblical principles about marriage and family, such as the permanence of the union, the importance of bearing and raising children, the necessity of employing loving discipline, and the involvement within a supportive religious community can all reinforce family cohesion.[6]

In their book *Becoming Spiritual Soulmates with Your Child* Robert and Debra Bruce state that—

- when both parents attend worship regularly, 72 percent of their children remain faithful later in life;
- when only Dad attends worship regularly, 55 percent of their children remain faithful;
- when only Mom attends worship regularly, 15 percent of their children remain faithful;
- when neither attends worship regularly, 6 percent of their children remain faithful.[7]

A great deal of research has confirmed the necessity of building strong families. Thus far the results have been very consistent. Yet we are just as consistent in ignoring the insights of that research. We must begin listening to what God is saying to us as a church and provide ministries that strengthen families. The chart "Family Growth Needs" in chapter 7, page 41, can help you identify needs that may exist in your church and community.

## God Speaks Through the Church

God also speaks to us by the Holy Spirit through His church, so it is important to listen to what God is saying through His people. God can speak to us through His church in several ways. One way is through those who join your church. Only God can draw persons to Himself through the Holy Spirit, and He does so through the church. Therefore, everyone who enters the family of God through our churches is a product of God's work. We need to listen to what God is saying and observe what He is doing through the individuals and families He brings into our churches.

God has an eternal plan for each person He draws into His family. Does your church attract a large number of young couples? Senior adults? Boomers? Busters? Down-and-outs? Up-and-outs? Notice where He is working and join Him in ministering to the families He is drawing to your church. He may bring some families there to teach you lessons in patience, long-suffering, or servanthood. He could provide individuals and families needed to conduct certain ministries. Whatever the case, be aware that when God draws a family to your church, He is speaking to you through His church.

> **Everyone who enters the family of God is a product of God's work**

Another way God speaks through the church is through your present membership. Do any families in your church fit these descriptions?

- A senior adult living alone
- A senior adult living with an adult child
- A childless couple
- A blended family
- A single-parent family
- A single parent without children living at home
- A single adult living alone
- A couple living together out of wedlock
- Other nontraditional families

The chart "Three Types of Families" on page 15 may help you understand the families in your church. At any given time in the life of the church you will find families in crisis, stable families, and growing families. Notice that the descriptions of these types of families vary tremendously. Also notice that each family's motivation differs according to their present situation or mind-set. On one end of the spectrum, pain and mere survival may motivate one family, while growth and the potential for a better life may motivate a family on the other end of the spectrum. A family in crisis needs someone to come alongside them and provide immediate support, intervention, and relief from the pain they are experiencing. They cannot make plans for tomorrow or dream of a future. They are just trying to make it through the next hour. In contrast, vibrant, growing families are constantly looking for ways to grow in their relationship with God and one another. Though they are very stable, they are unsatisfied with remaining where they are in life. They know their future can be even better than their present.

Here is the ministry challenge. As you examine the chart, jot down the names of families in your church who fit each family type. You will also discover that the lines between these categories are fluid. A growing family in your church may find themselves in the midst of a crisis and in need of immediate attention. However, the growing family is able to move through the crisis and become stronger. For the family that exists in a constant state of crisis, this becomes just another incident to keep them down. The greatest challenge lies in ministry to stable families, which make up the majority of your church. The struggle with ministering to this group is that they neither recognize the need nor desire to change. Examine this chart closely and pray for the families you know who fall into the categories presented. You may need to design ministries that help address the needs of families in each category. If you hear God speaking to you about the needs of one or more of these groups of families, carefully listen to what He is saying through the church.

Have you recently asked your church members what their needs and interests are? This is another way God speaks through His church to reveal Himself, His purposes, and His ways. You can use "Needs and Interests Survey" in chapter 7, beginning on page 43, or you may also order this survey in a computer-scored format from LifeWay Christian Resources.[8] After you have received the results of the survey, you can use "Needs and Interests Survey Planning Sheet," described on page 47, to assess the information you gather and to plan ways to join God in ministering to families in your church.

**Be sensitive to persons God places in your path who may share a burden for families**

Remember that you are not the only one in your church to whom God speaks about family needs or concerns. God can and will speak through others in your congregation. Allow God an opportunity to speak through His people by asking the congregation what their needs and interests are. Also be sensitive to persons God places in your path who may share a burden for families in your church and community. As you proceed through this resource, pray for God to reveal these persons to you as you strive to obey Him in ministering to families.

[1]Henry T. Blackaby and Claude V. King, *Experiencing God: Knowing and Doing the Will of God* (Nashville: LifeWay, 1990), 20.

[2]Henry T. Blackaby and Claude V. King, *The Experiencing God Study Bible* (Nashville: Broadman & Holman, 1994), 3.

[3]Avery T. Willis Jr., *MasterLife 1: The Disciple's Cross* (Nashville: LifeWay, 1996), 55.

[4]T. W. Hunt and Catherine Walker, *Disciple's Prayer Life: Walking in Fellowship with God* (Nashville: LifeWay, 1997), 63.

[5]Jerrold K. Footlick, as quoted by Stuart Briscoe and Mel Lawrenz, "What Pastors Can Do to Strengthen Families," *Marriage and Family: A Christian Journal*, vol. 1, issue 1 (1997), 70.

[6]George Barna, *The Future of the American Family* (Chicago: Moody, 1993), 198–99.

[7]Robert and Debra Bruce, *Becoming Spiritual Soulmates with Your Child* (Nashville: Broadman & Holman, 1996), 52.

[8]Order by writing to Phil Waugh, MSN 151; LifeWay Christian Resources; 127 Ninth Avenue, North; Nashville, TN 37234; by calling (615) 251-2275; or by emailing *phil.waugh@lifeway.com*.

# Three Types of Families

| | Family in Crisis | Stable Family | Growing Family |
|---|---|---|---|
| **Description** | Crisis<br><br>**Remedial** (takes apart, analyzes, puts back together)<br><br>**Medical model** (fix it)<br><br>Healing-oriented<br><br>Intervention needed<br><br>Therapy<br><br>Counseling<br><br>Problem solving<br><br>Relieving pressure<br><br>Sickness<br><br>Mending, repairing<br><br>High risk | Coping<br><br>Preventive<br><br>Solid<br><br>Stable<br><br>Satisfactory<br><br>"Average"<br><br>"Normal"<br><br>"Good"<br><br>Comfortable<br><br>Low risk | Growing<br><br>Educational<br><br>Enriching<br><br>Enhancing<br><br>Maximizing potential<br><br>Strength building<br><br>Intentional<br><br>Seeking fulfillment<br><br>Confident<br><br>Some risk |
| **Motivation** | **Pain** (survival) | **Existence** (get by) | **Growth** (potential) |
| **Family Focus** | Immediate (hour by hour) | Day by day<br>Sunday by Sunday | Tomorrow<br>What the future holds |
| **Stability/ Satisfaction Factor** | Unstable/ unsatisfied | | Stable/ unsatisfied |

Unstable/ satisfied      Stable/ satisfied

# Chapter 2

# A Foundation for Family Ministry

The formula for success in family ministry is to see where God is working and join Him. Unless God builds the house, we labor in vain (see Ps. 127:1). He is the Master Builder, and we are laborers with Him. Our eyes need to be on God and His activity.

As God reveals to you where He is working among families in your church and community, He will invite you to join Him in one or more of the following areas of ministry: prevention, enrichment, intervention, and/or outreach. These four areas of ministry form the foundational support you offer families. What you do in these four areas of ministry reveals what you believe about God and His heart for families.

A closer look at each area of ministry will reveal what each has to offer families.

## Prevention

Prevention ministries focus on helping individuals, couples, and families prepare for the future. The best preventative to the deterioration of the family is God's presence in the family. Positive change can take place when we allow God's influence to permeate our families. The best time to stop the deterioration of the family is before it starts. Each family needs God's presence at the center of the home, but He has to be invited. The church plays an important role in leading couples and families to discover this truth.

> **The best preventative to the deterioration of the family is God's presence in the family**

One way a church can join God in the ministry of prevention is through premarital counseling or marriage preparation. When a couple comes to the ministerial staff of your church to be married, several procedures should already be in place that can be initiated immediately.

1. When the couple requests to be married, they should be given the Covenant Marriage policy of your church. How is this preventative in nature? It begins the process of educating the couple on the value of a covenant marriage and the importance your church places on such a union.

2. When the couple sets a date for their wedding, their names should be given to those responsible for the prayer ministry of your church. Prayer can play a vital role in preparing the couple for their future together.

3. The couple should enroll in marriage-preparation classes, allowing enough time between sessions to process the information and skills being taught. An excellent resource to assist in this ministry is *Counsel for the Nearly and Newly Married.* You may also want to provide a study of *I Take Thee to Be My Spouse* during the Sunday School hour (see "Ministry Resources," beginning on p. 57).

Other examples of prevention ministries are personal-growth groups, preparing for a blended family, preparing for adoption, preparing for the first child, prenatal care, childbirth classes, parental instruction and personality assessments, and preretirement assistance to the families in your church and community.

## Enrichment

Strengthening families in daily living is important. Enrichment ministries focus on the family's nurture and growth. The various events, studies, and resources provided in this area of ministry are designed to enhance and/or strengthen an individual, a couple, or a family.

Instilling in family members' hearts and minds the importance of building their home on the foundation of Jesus Christ is essential. Providing family members a biblical understanding of God's intent for marriage and family is a beginning point in this process. This understanding comes about when the Holy Spirit reveals God's purposes for the family. This can occur when individuals are provided the right information and are able to assimilate and apply the information in life situations. We grow in our family relationships in direct proportion to our relationship with God. He expects us to grow in all aspects of our being.

> **God expects us to grow in all aspects of our being.**

Although not designed as preventatives or tools of intervention, enrichment opportunities offer help to families in charting their course through the developmental stages of life and even as they face more acute family crises. They can be used to strengthen the foundation of the home so that it withstands the storms of life. Enrichment opportunities can also be used to intervene in developmental crises that occur during stages of growth such as the teenage years. By helping people develop new insights and skills in anticipation of coming life transitions, you can equip them with tools to enhance their growth and can defuse potentially destructive responses to change.

Consider offering courses of study that assist families in identifying realistic objectives, learning new skills and techniques to accomplish those objectives, and applying the new insights in their relationships. Topics may include family communication, conflict resolution, money management, Christian sex education, marriage enrichment, parenting, preparation for retirement, and caring for aging parents. See "Family Enrichment Study Plan" below for a suggested annual plan for family enrichment.

Additional opportunities for enrichment come in the form of events. Designed for single adults, married couples, and senior adults, these enrichment events cover a broad range of topics and concerns (see "Ministry Resources," beginning on p. 57).

# Family Enrichment Study Plan

| | September | December | January | March | May | June |
|---|---|---|---|---|---|---|
| **Marriage Track** | Covenant Marriage: Partnership and Commitment or Communication and Intimacy: Covenant Marriage | The Five Love Languages | New Faces in the Frame: A Guide to Marriage and Parenting in the Blended Family | Making Love Last Forever | Experiencing God as Couples | The Three Chairs: Experiencing Spiritual Breakthroughs |
| **Parenting Track** | Parenting by Grace: Discipline and Spiritual Growth or ParentProject | The Five Love Languages of Children | Shaping the Next Generation | Building Strong Families | Experiencing God or Truth Matters … for You and Tomorrow's Generation | Empowered Parenting or New Faces in the Frame: A Guide to Marriage and Parenting in the Blended Family |

# Intervention

The chart "Three Types of Families" (p. 15) highlighted the fact that some families seem to remain in a constant state of emergency, while others experience a crisis in their lives but are able to grow from it. Intervention ministries intervene in a situation to assist in immediate and ongoing change in the individual or family unit. Intervention provides tangible help and hope to individual family members and family units in times of extreme stress and need. You may need to lead the church in establishing policies for this particular area of ministry. Your church will need to decide the type and degree of intervention it can offer.

The church's call to this form of ministry can be seen in the account of Jesus' raising Lazarus from the dead (see John 11:38-44). Jesus asked the crowd that had gathered to mourn with Mary and Martha to do two things. First He told them to roll away the stone. After He had raised Lazarus, Jesus called on the crowd to unwrap the grave clothes. As Christians we are all called to do those same things. We are to remove the obstacles that hinder individuals, couples, and their families from coming to the Lord. And we are to help unwrap those who are saved through faith in Jesus Christ but are still bound by the "grave clothes" of problems, crises, and unresolved issues. Most churches do an effective job of intervention in cases of death and hospitalization but beyond these arenas may become uncomfortable and negligent. The church needs to be sensitive to the scope and variety of ways families experience crises and thus need someone to intervene on their behalf.

**Be sensitive to the ways families experience crises**

You may also want to consider joining God in ministering to the needs of families facing specific and significant transitional periods in their lives as well as acute crises. Examples of ministry opportunities to meet these needs include—

- becoming a mentor couple for newly married couples;
- providing care for and celebrating the birth of a new baby;
- regularly visiting and ministering to homebound persons;
- ministering to the hospitalized and their families;
- providing a ministry of care to families who are bereaved.[1]

In cases in which ongoing assistance is needed, the church can offer support groups that address the specific needs God reveals through the circumstances faced by families in your church and community. Some examples are grief recovery, divorce recovery, ministry to families of persons with AIDS, ministry to parents of teens, alcohol addiction, single parenting, making peace with the past, recovering from sexual abuse, overcoming sexual addictions, recovering from substance abuse, and coping with terminal illness. Support groups provide a safe place for those who share similar hurts and experience similar circumstances. LIFE Support resources can be used in support groups to address many of these issues (see "Ministry Resources," beginning on p. 57).

In addition to conducting support groups, your church may want to—

- offer professional counseling;
- provide referral services;
- offer your church facility as a meeting place for a substance-abuse support group or another support group;
- sponsor a halfway house;
- sponsor a home for unwed mothers;
- provide a clothes closet or food pantry.

In Matthew 25 we are taught that wherever there are human needs, God is present. However, we should be sensitive to God's speaking to us by the Holy Spirit. For when the Holy Spirit quickens our spirit to the needs of an individual, a couple, or a family, that is His invitation for us to join God in meeting that particular need. No matter what means are used to minister to the needs of families in crisis, the church is always encouraged to—

- be accessible and take appropriate initiative;
- show genuine concern;
- be worthy of trust;
- demonstrate warmth and acceptance.[2]

# Outreach

Outreach ministries equip, challenge, and provide tools for families, parents, or couples to reach beyond their families to minister to families in their community.

To illustrate the challenges and opportunities facing churches in reaching out to families who need the Lord, let me share two stories from the life of Linda Ranson-Pallemino, a single parent.

After my divorce I joined a church that had a singles group. After we had been attending this church for awhile, my son's Bible study teacher came to visit him. We were working in the yard and my son invited this young man to join us on the patio. I remember thinking, "how nice, this is the first time someone at church has reached out to my son." As we all three sat visiting, the Bible study teacher began to share about his class. "These kids from broken homes just destroy my class." I looked at my son and he had the most shocked look on his face and I got a knot in the pit of my stomach. He went on to say, "They don't come very often and when they do come, they don't know what's going on and they are troublemakers. I don't know why they can't come every Sunday. It would sure make my job easier." At some point in this conversation my son got up and ran out of the yard. I mumbled something to the effect of "Do you not understand you're sitting in the yard of a single parent family?" He didn't realize that, because he thought Brian was a very nice kid and didn't give him any problems. He wondered why Brian only came about every other Sunday.

> My heart ached for my son. As a young teen, he was driven away from a church

I could not ever pull my son back into that church. Oh, he went every Sunday that he was home but it was a struggle. My heart ached for my son. As a young teen, he was driven away from a church.

The second story is quite different. A few years later, I had the opportunity to be called to a church as a church pianist. After we had been attending for several months they made an announcement one Sunday morning that the annual father/son fishing trip was coming up. As they made the announcement, I felt that knot coming up in the pit of my stomach again. Brian wasn't with me that Sunday morning and after church one of the men came up to me and asked me, "Is Brian going to the father/son fishing trip?" I said, "I guess you don't know that Brian doesn't have a father at home." He said to me, "I guess you don't know I have three daughters and no son at home." "Oh, I didn't know that." He then asked if he could adopt my son for that weekend. I asked him to call my son that evening and ask him.

To make a long story short, on Friday I took a very apprehensive young man to church. Saturday evening when he returned home he was quite a different young man. He was so excited. "Mom, guess what? I got to go fishing in a boat. And at night, they invited me to sit around the campfire with them. And you know what else? They gave me coffee to drink!" This group of Christian men did something that I as a single mom couldn't do. They brought my son back into the folds of a loving New Testament church. In one weekend they brought my son back to the Lord. They built a relationship with a young man that has never been forgotten.[3]

Both of these churches had an opportunity to reach out and minister to the needs of a family in need. Only one of them did so effectively. And it was accomplished through a fishing trip.

Most single-parent families need the support and care of the church family. However, do not assume that a single-parent family should always stay on the receiving end. Single-parent families have the same call to reach out to others that other families have. However, this call is often stifled by the demands of their jobs and families.

> When determining if a church wants to develop a ministry for single parent families there are two components to be considered. Like any other ministry in a church the first component to developing this ministry must be prayer. The second component in this type of ministry is education about the single parent family. Churches are just now beginning to realize that single adults with children are a family. Many people don't realize that single parent families experience several phases or stages in their journey to becoming a healthy single parent family. Misunderstandings regarding this process of the single parent family can be detrimental to not only the church but also to the very people the church is trying to reach, the single parent family.[4]

Another example of outreach ministry is related to the Covenant Marriage policy. Your church can equip older, more spiritually mature Christian couples to mentor newlywed couples. This practice allows couples to minister directly to other couples and helps reduce the divorce rate in your church and in our nation. Mentoring has proved to have a higher success rate than any form of marriage counseling.

Another opportunity for outreach is to offer studies of *Marriage Savers* by Michael McManus (Zondervan, 1993), which will lead your church to develop covenants with other churches in your community to establish criteria for couples desiring to be married in those churches. By reaching out to other churches and organizations in the community and developing a Community Marriage Covenant, you provide a network of support for couples in your community through a Covenant Marriage environment.

Encourage the families in your church to reach out to their community. *Family to Family* is a resource that can be used to help families identify their uniqueness, write a family mission statement, and then operate from that statement (see "Ministry Resources," beginning on p. 57). Introduce families to family outreach by involving them in a silent prayer walk through their neighborhoods. As they walk through their neighborhoods, they can pray for the families in each house and for the families that will move into the neighborhood. Next, they can leave a *Choice Creations* tract pertaining to family issues or a *HomeLife, BabyLife, ParentLife,* or *Living with Teenagers* magazine with their neighbors and invite them to church (see "Ministry Resources," beginning on p. 57). Finally, they can invite their neighbors to their homes for fellowship, witness, and encouragement.

**Encourage the families in your church to reach out to their community**

Outreach allows churches to introduce Christian values and biblical truths to the broader community through home-study groups, community-action projects, and missions. Through outreach not only can God influence society through us by our intentional ministry to families within the local church and the broader secular community, but He also can and will influence society for generations to come.

Your church can sponsor relevant, life-changing seminars and conferences in community centers, in apartment complexes, or in church members' homes.

Offer the families in your church opportunities to serve their community. A church in Alabama hosts boys and girls from a local child-care facility from Saturday morning through Sunday afternoon during the Christmas season. The purpose of this ministry is to join God in ministering to the needs of children who are separated from their own families for various reasons. The host family makes these children a part of their home for these hours. Family members do not buy gifts but share themselves and their time—especially the adult family members. Participants are single adults, young couples without children, families with children, and older couples with grown children.

Families can also become personally involved in missions through giving and going. When one family member goes on a mission trip, it affects the entire family. What if entire families went on mission trips? Another option is for families to adopt missionary families with children the approximate ages of theirs and provide ongoing encouragement and support. For additional missions opportunities, contact the North American Mission Board; 4200 North Point Parkway; Alpharetta, GA 30022-4174; (770) 410-6000 or the International Mission Board; P.O. Box 6767; Richmond, VA 23230; (804) 353-0151.

Resources your church can use in each of these areas of family ministry can be found in chapter 8, beginning on page 48.

If your ministry to families is to be effective, it must be purpose-directed. The purpose of family ministry is to join God in ministering to the needs of families by intentionally providing a focused ministry of prevention, enrichment, intervention, and outreach. After you have determined where God wants you to join Him in ministering to the needs of the families in your church and community, you may want to develop a plan that includes these four areas. What you do reveals what you believe about God and His desire for families. Be intentional in your focus and be open to God's direction. Always be prepared to make adjustments to join God wherever He is working in the families of your church and community.

> **What you do reveals what you believe about God and His desire for families**

---

[1]John M. Lepper Jr., *When Crisis Comes Home* (Nashville: Convention, 1992), 141.
[2]Ibid., 148–52.
[3]Linda Ranson-Pallemino, "Bind Up the Broken Hearted: A challenge for churches regarding single parent family ministries," unpublished paper. Used by permission.
[4]Ibid.

# The Focus of Family Ministry

According to George Barna in his book *The Future of the American Family*, a church's focus needs to be on teaching God's view of family as opposed to the world's toleration and acceptance of any lifestyle. The church needs to support families on all fronts. The church is the only institution that speaks out for family values and the need for those values to be biblically based and Christ-centered.[1] For too long the church has sacrificed truth on the altar of tolerance. We have allowed the worldview to penetrate the church rather than allowing God's view to penetrate the world.

Focus is necessary to family ministry. Focus gives direction to ministry and makes planning efficient. Focus prevents the waste of precious resources and increases the effectiveness of family ministry. But we must make sure that we focus on the right things. Too often we take the "Ready, fire, aim" approach to ministry. With good intentions we prepare our ammunition, fire our guns, look to see what we hit, then go and draw a bull's-eye around it.

> The focus of family ministry needs to be on joining God where He is working in families

We cannot take this approach and ask God to bless what we are doing. Do you remember the way God blessed Adam and Eve and Abraham? The focus of family ministry needs to be on joining God where He is working in the families of your church and community. He will bless that which He initiates. For instance, if you believe that only God can draw people to Himself, focus on what kind of families He is bringing into your church. If certain families have similar needs, join God in meeting those needs.

## Write a Mission Statement

Does your church have a vision statement or a mission statement? Many churches have such statements. The intent of these statements is to affirm our identity as God's people, establish core values, and set directions for our church based on who we are and what God has called us to do.

As you establish a family ministry, your focus should not be on church programs but on ministering to the needs of families in keeping with your church's mission statement. One way you can achieve this goal is to develop a mission statement that directs all you do in family ministry. You might want to call this a mission statement, but make sure it is based on what God is doing rather than what you plan to do for God. This statement needs to reflect what you believe that God is inviting the church to do to join Him in meeting the needs of families.

To develop a mission statement for family ministry, you must first affirm where you see God working in the lives of individuals, couples, and families. After you have identified where you see God working, then you can develop a broad, brief statement of the focus of your church's ministry to families. It is to be carefully and succinctly written to communicate God's purpose for your church's ministry to families. As you write this mission statement, you will want to ask yourself these questions.

- Does it reflect where you see God working?
- Does it focus on joining God in ministering to the needs of families?
- Does it present a biblical view of the family?
- Does it raise the ideal for families according to God's Word?
- Does it meet the needs of families from a biblical viewpoint?

• Does it demonstrate God's love to the families in your church and community whose needs vary from critical intervention to outreach opportunities?

## Sample Mission Statement

We believe that God is drawing His people back to a biblical understanding and practice of marriage as a covenant relationship.

## List Purpose Statements

After affirming God's activity and developing your mission statement that defines the way you will join His activity, the next step is to develop specific statements of purpose for your ministry. Such statements bring greater focus to the mission statement by answering the question "Why are we doing what we are doing?" These statements might include the following.
 • To educate persons about God's design for marriage and family life
 • To equip persons in relationship-building skills
 • To inform families of the needs and interests of the broader church family
 • To support families who have special needs and concerns
 • To reach out in Christ's love to the families in the community
 • To unite with other churches to support marriage and family issues
 • To develop church policies on marriage and family issues

As you formulate your mission statement and begin developing your purpose statements, you will need to define exactly what your philosophy of family ministry will be. In doing so, you will formulate the principles that will govern the church's programs in family ministry. You will need to consider areas like the following.
 • Your beliefs about marriage
 • Your beliefs about divorce
 • Your position on marriage preparation
 • Your part in training men for their roles as husbands and fathers
 • Your part in training women for their roles as wives and mothers
 • The role therapy should play in the ministry
 • Your role in developing programs for divorced individuals
 • Strategies for training people
 • Your position on family advocacy
 • Your position on the use of government agencies

Sample purpose statements based on the previous mission statement might be the following.

## Sample Purpose Statements

 • We will educate our congregation about the need to establish a Covenant Marriage Policy that provides guidelines for the congregation and the ministerial staff in regard to marriages performed in the church and/or by our ministerial staff.
 • We will provide ongoing ministries to couples who seek to establish and grow in their covenant marriages.
 • Where possible in keeping with our doctrinal beliefs and our mission statement, we will join other congregations in our community to strengthen the fabric of our society by uplifting marriage as a covenant.

# Determine Your Goals

After you have established your mission statement and have written purpose statements, you need to determine the specific outcomes you would like to see achieved in the foreseeable future—both long- and short-range. Your goals seek to answer the question "How will we accomplish the mission God is leading us to pursue?" Take, for example, the purpose statement "We will lead the congregation in establishing a Covenant Marriage Policy that provides guidelines for the congregation and the ministerial staff in regard to marriages performed in the church and/or by our ministerial staff." Some goals would include the following.

## Sample Goals

- *First year.* Present a Covenant Marriage Policy to the congregation for its consideration and approval as a church body.
- *Second year.* Begin a ministry of marriage preparation for engaged couples based on the Covenant Marriage Policy.
- *Third year.* Begin introducing ongoing ministries to couples in the church and community that communicate your commitment to them and to Covenant Marriage.

## State Your Objectives

Next, write what you will do to reach your family-ministry goals. "Objectives are statements about what has to be done to reach the goals."[2] For example, if you set a first-year goal of presenting a Covenant Marriage Policy to the congregation, you would include some of the following objectives.

## Sample Objectives

- *0–2 months.* Gather existing information from other churches and the national Covenant Marriage office about marriage/wedding policies.
- *2–4 months.* Evaluate your church's present policies in light of those you have collected from other churches and information received from the Covenant Marriage Movement office.
- *Month 4.* Present the vision of developing the Covenant Marriage Policy to the congregation, giving your reasons for it.
- *4–6 months.* Develop a working draft of a Covenant Marriage Policy to present to the congregation. Make sure it represents a comprehensive ministry and is presented for input by the congregation.
- *Month 6.* Present the working draft of the Covenant Marriage Policy to the church for its input.
- *6–8 months.* Finalize the Covenant Marriage Policy to present to the congregation for approval.
- *Month 8.* Call for a church vote for final approval of the policy.
- *8–12 months.* Begin developing an implementation plan to initiate the marriage ministry based on the policy.

---

[1]George Barna, *The Future of the American Family* (Chicago: Moody, 1993), 208.
[2]Charles M. Sell, *Family Ministry* (Grand Rapids: Zondervan, 1995), 361.

# A Process for Family Ministry

# Chapter 4

God pursues a continuing love relationship with us that is real and personal.[1] One arena in which God does this is the family. Therefore, you have an opportunity to join Him in this endeavor. You have an opportunity to serve God in providing family-ministry events, programs, studies, and activities that train, equip, and encourage family members to relate to one another in ways that honor God.

Granted, building a family ministry is no easy task. It's not like building a prefab playhouse or tree house. It is more like constructing a permanent residence in which you and your family will live. Charles Swindoll in his book *Strike the Original Match* states that a time may come in a marriage when you are faced with a remodeling project. He writes: "There are four things nobody can deny who has endured remodeling:
1. It takes longer than you planned.
2. It costs more than you figured.
3. It is messier than you anticipated.
4. It requires greater determination than you expected."[2]

The same can be said about family life in general and about constructing a family ministry to meet the needs of families in your church and community. It will require an enormous amount of energy, but with God as your strength and guide, you will discover an untapped reservoir of energy and motivation to complete the task. Like the psalmist, you need to

> Commit your way to the Lord,
> Trust also in Him, and He will do it (Ps. 37:5, NASB).

This is not your house, your ministry. You are not the owner or the architect; therefore, you are not expected to have all of the answers and to know every nook and cranny in the house. You and other leaders need to look to the Lord and to trust in Him and His direction. He will lead you where you need to be. The psalmist's admonition is reiterated in Proverbs 16:2-3:

> All the ways of a man are clean in his own sight,
> But the Lord weighs the motives.
> Commit your works to the Lord
> And your plans will be established (NASB).

The psalmist also wrote:

> Unless the Lord builds the house,
> They labor in vain who build it (Ps. 127:1, NASB).

**God expects us to come to Him for direction in building family ministry**

The psalmist requested that God "teach us to number our days" (Ps. 90:12, NASB). We are to plan each day with God's priorities in mind.

Godly leaders live by these principles. God expects us to come to Him for direction in building family ministry, and He expects us to be obedient in following the plans He lays out for His church. He is the Master Builder, and we are His colaborers.

This resource can serve as a blueprint to assist you in building your ministry, as one plan to help you and your church keep on track in ministering to families in your church and community. If at any point in the building process the Master Builder appears to change the plans, trust Him to lead you because He has the master plan. He knows where He wants you to join Him, and He has the power and resources to bring about His purposes. He knows what He wants His house to look like and how He wants it to be used. Yet the Master Builder allows us to participate in the building process.

## Phases in the Building Process

*Phase 1: Determine what God is saying to you and your church about ministering to families and respond.* More often than not, the phrase "Don't just stand there; do some-

> **Stop long enough to determine what God is saying**

thing" characterizes our approach to ministering to the needs of families. However, a more intentional and productive approach to ministering to the needs of families should begin from the standpoint characterized by the statement "Don't just do something; stand there." In other words, you need to " 'be still, and know that I am God' " (Ps. 46:10, NIV). Stop long enough to determine what God is saying to your church about ministering to families.

Do you recall from chapter 1 the four avenues through which God speaks to us? God speaks by the Holy Spirit through the Bible, prayer, circumstances, and the church to reveal Himself, His purposes, and His ways. Continue praying that God will speak to you through these avenues as you discern where He wants you to join Him in meeting the needs of families in and through your church.

If God brings a need to your attention, that becomes your personal invitation to join Him in meeting the need. He may not be inviting the pastor or a Sunday School teacher or a fellow Christian to meet that need. You can't necessarily count on God's speaking to everyone else as He is speaking to you. When God speaks to you, you are the one who needs to respond to His invitation. He will not invite you to join Him in a task for which He will not provide everything necessary to complete it. You may initially be the only one doing family ministry, but remember that God, who has always been working around you, will provide for your every need. God always anoints that which He initiates.

If you are the only one God has spoken to about this ministry, begin asking Him to raise up others to join you. Pray for Him to guide you in identifying individuals who have a strong desire to minister to families. God may already be at work in the lives of others, impressing on them the need for this ministry. As you identify these individuals, ask them to pray with you for the families in your church. Let God speak to them as He has spoken to you. When God speaks to them, that becomes their invitation to join Him as you have joined Him. In so doing, God will pool your resources, gifts, and passions for family ministry. You can then join together in praying for the families in your church by name. You can also begin praying together for God's revelation of where He is working in the families in your church and community. Begin now to list the names of individuals God places on your heart during prayer or places in your path who share a burden for families or a call to family ministry.

If God has already brought several of you together, begin praying for one another's families. Divide the names of the families in your church and spend time in consecrated prayer for them. You may wish to begin with an informal group, maybe a committee, to join you in this endeavor, or you may wish to adopt a formal organization. If you choose the former option, this committee can provide selected family-ministry opportunities prior to adopting a formal organization.

You may begin your ministry to families at this point or, having already established a successful family ministry, you may wish to adopt a more formal organization. See chapter 5, "A Form for Family Ministry," for guidance in accomplishing this phase in the building process.

***Phase 2: Determine where God wants you to join Him.*** Not only does God speak through His Word and prayer, but He also speaks through circumstances and His people. One of the best ways to determine where God wants you to join Him is to ask His people to share what is taking place in their lives and in the lives of those in the community. What is God doing in the lives of individuals, couples, parents, and children? Specific needs exist in the families in your church and community that God desires to meet. Help church members and leaders

**Specific needs exist in families that God desires to meet**

understand the importance of families and the value of ministering to their needs. The needs are countless, but God will direct you to those He wants to meet through your church.

Families in North America have experienced and are experiencing drastic changes. Churches are overwhelmed by the needs of families. Begin noticing medical reports on family needs. Compile newspaper and magazine articles that report on family breakup and family needs. Share these with other concerned individuals and church leaders.

Obtain the family statistics for your community from a source like your county health department or public library. Assess the circumstances in your community and state. Share this information with your church through means like posters, newsletters, and video monitors. List any family statistics, people groups, or trends God is revealing to you as opportunities for ministry.

Remember, those of us in the church are not immune to these unprecedented changes. No church is any stronger than its families. As we shape the family, we are also shaping the church. And we certainly need to shape our churches so that they shape healthy families.

As you assess the circumstances and needs of families, you will find that at some point in time, all families will face one or all four of these categories of need or issues.
  • Acute crises such as divorce, death, and hospitalization
  • Developmental needs such as retirement, the birth of a baby, and adolescence
  • Life issues and stresses such as blending families, life as a single parent, busy travel schedules, communication, developing intimacy with spouse, and parenting
  • Spiritual needs such as salvation, Christian maturity, witnessing, and missions

The church has been given the unique responsibility and privilege of providing a nurturing, sheltering environment for the formation and development of family.

***Phase 3: Assess the needs of families in your church and community.*** In the book *Family Enrichment in Your Church* Gary Hauk suggested several ways to determine the needs of families. Each of these can provide a unique snapshot of the needs of families in your church and community. Here are some ways to determine needs.

1. Ask church leaders, such as the youth minister, the minister to adults, Bible-study teachers, senior-adult leaders, and so on, to share what their needs are and what they hear from their respective groups. Ask if they would be willing to help you gather information to use in ministering to the needs of families.

2. Conducting a family census will help you determine the number of family units in your church. It will also help you learn other facts about the families in your church, such as family configurations, the number of young couples, the number of families with adolescents, and so on. Use the information in "Family Demographics" in chapter 7, page 40, to help you gather this information.

3. Examine family growth needs. Looking at families in various stages will help you gain a better understanding of their needs. Use the chart "Family Growth Needs" in chapter 7, page 41, to assist you with this task.

4. Taking a needs and interests survey can give you a comprehensive view of families and their perspectives. Use "Needs and Interests Survey" in chapter 7,

beginning on page 43. You may wish to adapt the survey for your own situation.

5. Conduct a Family Needs Forum, which is a guided discussion with a small group of people. Individuals are asked to identify needs and issues faced by people in their church and community. These individuals then commit to pray for God to reveal how He wants to meet these needs and address these issues through your church. A good way to provide this opportunity is through the Bible-study organization.[3] This idea is described more fully in chapter 7, pages 40–43.

*Phase 4: Evaluate existing resources in your church and community and make adjustments.* Before you begin the serious task of planning family-ministry events and programs in your church, stop and determine the resources that are already available to you. In this way you can better match available resources to the needs of families in your church and community. Resources come in various forms. Consider print, people, time, monetary, and spiritual resources. How is God presently ministering to families through your church and community?

Every church provides a ministry to families. What is your church already doing? Even if you do not have a separate and intentional family-ministry program, your church probably cares about families. Evaluate your existing family-ministry provisions and programs. Remember that family ministry is more than a base program. As such, it can utilize other organizations as vehicles through which to accomplish its tasks. Use the chart "Evaluating and Assisting Church Programs to Minister to Family Members" in chapter 8, page 56, to evaluate what your church is currently doing for families.

Also consider what is being done for families in your community, such as estate planning, investment services, child care, adult care, and so forth. Use the chart "Community Resources for Meeting Needs" in chapter 8, page 60, to discover community provisions for families. What needs are already being met? What adjustments need to be made in what your church is offering to meet the needs of families?

*Phase 5: Determine specific objectives.* What is God inviting you to join Him in doing? In this phase you join God's ministry to families in your church and community. If you followed the suggestions in phase 3, God has revealed to you the needs of families in your church and community. Having followed the suggestions in phase 4, you have a sense of the ministries and programs God has provided. You are now ready to join God in the direction He wants to take in ministering to families in your church and community.

Don't become overwhelmed by the needs you have discovered. The needs are great, but God is greater. He "will supply all your needs according to His riches in glory" (Phil. 4:19, NASB). Instead of trying to meet all needs based on your own power, ask God which needs He wants to meet through you. This will require developing priorities. It will require saying no to some things in order to say yes to other things. You will need to stay close to your guide, the Holy Spirit, asking for discernment to choose the best course. Always keep in mind that if you can do it on your own might and by your own means, then it doesn't require faith in God to accomplish.

**The needs are great, but God is greater**

*Phase 6: Select programs, projects, events, and activities that will glorify God and will accomplish your stated objectives.* Design ministries to meet the priority needs of the families in your church and community. What is needed? When is it needed? Who needs it? Seek church approval, according to proper procedures, for the programs, projects, events, and activities you plan.

Review "Needs and Interests Survey" (beginning on p. 43) or other data you have gained in assessing needs. As you do this, you might like to brainstorm actions the church could take. Begin to determine which program you will use to meet needs or address issues. Match available resources to specific needs you have discovered.

*Phase 7: Promote the selected programs, projects, events, and activities.* Communicate to church members and leaders what is available to help meet the identified family-ministry needs. Make promotion positive, caring, and enthusiastic. See chapter 9, page 61, for ideas.

*Phase 8: Implement the programs, projects, events, and activities you perceive God is leading you to do.* Joining God in implementing the selected activities will require some adjustments in how you do things. "Family Ministry Time Line" on page 30 will help you begin your implementation and determine who needs to be involved. Learn as you go. Don't be discouraged when you need to make changes.

*Phase 9: Celebrate and evaluate the effectiveness of the programs, projects, events, and activities and continue the process.* Recognize the great things God has done. Sometimes we are so intent on providing ministries that we forget to celebrate what God has done. It is important to give those who have benefited from the ministry an opportunity to celebrate. During the celebration don't forget to thank the individuals God has used to provide the ministry.

Evaluation is one of the most strategic and yet often most neglected steps in the administrative process. After you have invested prayer and energy in a project, look objectively at the results. Was God in it? Did the program, project, event, or activity glorify God? Did it meet the needs God revealed to you? If so, ask yourself, *Where does God want our church to join Him next in ministering to the needs of families?*

> **Evaluation is one of the most strategic and yet often most neglected steps**

God doesn't want you to rest on past successes. Celebrate God's activity and build on the experience by beginning the process again. You may or may not need to discover needs again. You may be able to begin with phase 6 to continue ministering to the needs of families.

If you did not meet the needs that were previously discovered, ask yourself: *Where did we miss the mark? Where did we misunderstand God's will?* Then seek clarification of what God is saying. You may need to adjust what you are doing to join God in another area in which He is working. Remember, He has the right to interrupt your agenda any time He desires.

It is easier just to hope we achieved our goals. However, feedback is the chief basis for improvement. Evaluation is essential to reshaping our methods and programs and to modifying our goals. Here are ways to evaluate the outcome of a ministry project.

- Attendance
- Informal questionnaire
- Interviews
- Committee evaluation identifying the positive and negative results

When we begin building a house, a projected completion date and a time line must be established to keep the building on schedule. The time line on page 30 provides you a schedule for tracking your progress in constructing a family ministry that will glorify the Master Builder. As you plan, remember that He has the right to interrupt you at any point in the building project.

---

[1]Henry T. Blackaby and Claude V. King, *Experiencing God: Knowing and Doing the Will of God* (Nashville: LifeWay, 1990), 20.
[2]Charles R. Swindoll, *Strike the Original Match* (Portland: Multnomah, 1980), 9–10.
[3]Gary Hauk, *Family Enrichment in Your Church* (Nashville: Convention, 1988), 48–65.

# Family Ministry Time Line

| | What | How | When | Who |
|---|---|---|---|---|
| **P R E P A R A T I O N** | 1. Determine what God is saying to you and your church about ministering to families and respond. | Pray for God's leadership. Study biblical teaching. Invite others to join you in making observations. Present to the staff. | 12–16 months before initiation | |
| | 2. Determine where God wants you to join Him. | Assess the need. Form and train a family-ministry committee and communicate with staff. | 8–12 months before initiation | |
| | 3. Assess the needs of families in your church and community. | Hold Family Needs Forum or survey family needs. Present findings to pastor. | 8–12 months before initiation | |
| | 4. Evaluate existing resources in your church and community and make adjustments. | Discover church and community resources. Begin organizing ministries. | 6–7 months before initiation | |
| | 5. Determine specific objectives. | Form and train family-ministry committee. Establish objectives. | 6–7 months before initiation | |
| **A C T I O N** | 6. Select appropriate programs, projects, events, and activities. | Develop annual plan to meet stated objectives. Present existing opportunities. Present ministry options. Train leaders. | 4–6 months before initiation | |
| | 7. Promote the selected programs, projects, events, and activities. | Communicate what God is doing. Promote events, programs, etc. | Launch (4–6 weeks long) at annual meeting, ongoing | |
| | 8. Implement the programs, projects, events, and activities. | Provide family ministry through new and existing programs. | Ongoing | |
| | 9. Celebrate and evaluate the effectiveness of the programs, projects, events, and activities and continue the process. | Add and delete ministries. Reach others. | 1 month after initiation, after major events, ongoing | |

# A Form for Family Ministry

Understanding the nature of family ministry is essential to understanding the form it should take in the church. Family ministry is not a base program of the church like worship or Bible study, because it doesn't have a specific, ongoing meeting time and place. Yet programs can be planned and implemented that meet the needs of families. Like evangelism, family ministry permeates all programs of the church. Therefore, if you are going to build a family ministry that will stand the test of time, you must look at every program of the church and ask yourself: *How does this program influence families? Are we building up and strengthening our families through this program or event?* Remember that an abundance of programs and activities doesn't necessarily equal effective family ministry.

## Getting Organized

Getting organized is not our ultimate goal. Our ultimate goal is to help families. The organization is not an end in itself but a means to an end. Getting organized is a needed task if we are to help families effectively. When we don't organize, our efforts are sporadic and haphazard at best. On the other hand, we don't want to be so organized that our attention is focused on keeping the organization running without paying attention to the actual ministries. Our

> **Getting organized is a needed task if we are to help families effectively**

goal is to help families, not create an organization. The organization, in whatever shape it takes, is a structure to plan, coordinate, and implement family ministry.

The structure or framework for family ministry might look different in different churches. Each church has been uniquely and wonderfully made by God to bring glory to Him and service to His people. In some cases you may be the organization! In other words, you may be the only person in your church who presently feels the call to join God in the area of family ministry. So begin by educating and encouraging the church on how family ministry can be done through your existing church structure.

Here are important questions to answer before you develop your organization.
• Who is responsible for enriching the lives of families?
• To whom is this person or group accountable?
• What are the specific responsibilities of the person or group responsible for enriching the lives of families?
• What does our overall organization look like to our church?
• How are decisions made and tasks accomplished in our church?
• What kind of family-ministry organization could best meet the needs of families and fit into our current church structure?

## Principles of Organization

*Adopt a structure that matches the structure of your church.* If you have a Church Council that is responsible for program planning, then the family-ministry coordinator needs to serve on the Church Council. If the pastor oversees all committees or programs, then the person and committee responsible for family ministry need to work directly with the pastor.

*Make sure family ministry focuses on providing ministries that conform to the mission statement.* Do not minimize the importance of any aspect of family ministry.

Churches need to take seriously their ministry to hurting families as well as provide enrichment for growing families.

*Develop prayer support.* One of the greatest ministries you can provide to families is prayer support. An active prayer ministry should be included in the organizational structure of your ministry to couples, parents, and their families.

*Develop a referral strategy.* Family-ministry events and programs, while offering positive and life-changing help to families, can also bring to a family's awareness the need for help that the provided programs and leaders are not equipped to handle. For example, a couple may be qualified to lead a marriage-enrichment workshop but may not have the ability or inclination to provide marriage counseling. A couple experiencing mild conflict may find that the conflict is intensified by open discussions during a marriage-enrichment weekend. The leader couple should be sensitive to this need and should be prepared to offer referral to a qualified marriage or family counselor.

> **One of the greatest ministries you can provide is prayer support**

When these situations arise, it is good to know when and how to refer individuals and couples to someone qualified to help them work through their difficulties. Some needs can best be met by a person or an agency especially prepared to provide specific types of assistance. Some psychological problems should be referred to a professionally trained counselor.

What will your strategy for referral be? Begin the referral process by telling the person of your inadequacy in that area of difficulty and by suggesting someone who can help.

Types of emotional difficulties that should be referred include the following.
- *Psychotic conditions.* Persons with psychotic conditions are losing touch with the real world and should be immediately referred to a counselor.
- *Neurotic reactions.* Neurotic reactions are milder types of emotional maladjustment than psychotic conditions. Individuals may be uncomfortable and perhaps distressed but are still capable of functioning in the real world.
- *Physiologically based conditions.* These conditions have their origins in body functions and may be attributed to such causes as chemical imbalances. Symptoms may include headaches, dizziness, fainting, loss of appetite, and so on.
- *Character disorders.* Individuals with these disorders are apparently devoid of a conscience or socially acceptable values.[1]

Talk with your pastor or a church-staff member to learn the way he would like for you to refer persons. Your church should keep a current list of Christian counselors or agencies in your community for reference.

You may need to seek biblical counselors, Christian counseling services, or counselors in your community to whom you can refer persons who are experiencing problems or conflicts. Ask them the following questions in an interview to help you determine whether their counseling fits your beliefs.
- What do you believe about God?
- What do you believe about humankind, human nature, sin, and its effect on our lives?
- What do you believe about marriage and divorce?
- What do you believe about the inspiration and reliability of Scripture in the context of your counseling and your clients' healing process?
- What do you believe about the gift of salvation and our responsibilities to God in our relationships with others?
- To what degree are you actively involved in a local congregation, and how are you serving Him in your family and church?
- What active counseling credentials do you presently hold?
- What professional organizations are you currently affiliated with?

In addition to these questions, you may want to contact the American Association of Christian Counselors at (804) 525-9470 for a list of counselors in your area who are affiliated with that organization. You will also want to learn whether other counseling-referral services are in your area, such as the Christian Counseling Center Referral Network in Boise, Idaho; (208) 343-0441; fax (208) 343-4993; *www.hope-healing.com*.

## Options for an Expanded Organization

Each organizational structure on the following chart begins with the same basic organization. The difference lies in the makeup of the family-ministry committee. The structure of your committee needs to reflect your ministry's goals and objectives.

| Organizing According to Needs and Interests | Organizing According to Program | Organizing According to Stages in the Family Life Cycle |
|---|---|---|
| Pastor/church staff<br>Church Council<br>Family-ministry coordinator<br>Family-ministry committee<br>• Marriage preparation<br>• Marriage enrichment<br>• Parent enrichment<br>• Blended families<br>• Support groups<br>• Single-parent families<br><br>Each area listed can be addressed by the larger family-ministry committee, or subcommittees can be formed with responsibility for each area. "Needs and Interests Survey" in chapter 7, page 43, is a valuable tool to use in organizing according to needs and interests. | Pastor/church staff<br>Church Council<br>Family-ministry coordinator<br>Family-ministry committee<br>• Ongoing programs such as an ongoing couples group<br>• Short-term programs such as marriage-enrichment weekends<br>• Joint programs like those jointly sponsored by other church-program organizations like discipleship training, Bible teaching, or Woman's Missionary Union<br>• Outreach programs such as a community couples event<br><br>Each way of programming can be addressed by the larger family-ministry committee or by subcommittees. Use "Evaluating and Assisting Church Programs to Minister to Family Members" in chapter 8, page 56, to organize according to programs. | Pastor/church staff<br>Church Council<br>Family-ministry coordinator<br>Family-ministry committee<br>• Premarriage and early marriage<br>• Early marriage/parenting years<br>• Families with adolescents<br>• Empty-nest years<br>• Retirement<br><br>"Family Growth Needs" in chapter 7, page 41, is a valuable tool to use in organizing according to stages in the family life cycle. |

## The Family-Ministry Committee

Family is important to everyone, no matter the family configuration or the degree of family health or dysfunction. But when everyone is responsible, few take this responsi-

**Create a position and a small group with the responsibility to enrich the lives of individuals and families**

bility seriously. Pastors may sometimes resist forming another committee or area of responsibility, fearing that it will add more work to their already full ministry. The idea is to create a position and a small group of persons with the responsibility to address the needs of individuals and families. Many churches call this the family-ministry committee under the leadership of a family-ministry coordinator. When churches have a functioning Church Council, the family-ministry coordinator serves on this program-planning group. In any case, the family-ministry coordinator needs to be a member of the group that plans the programs and develops the church calendar.

Someone on the church staff needs to serve as the administrator of the family-ministry committee. If this job should be assigned to the staff person responsible for pastoral care and counseling, then personal and family counseling should be restricted to a minimum. The counseling ministry should not interfere with the family minister's involvement in the educational and prevention programs that are so crucial. If the staff person has responsibilities for the family-life center, these responsibilities should not overshadow or take precedence over the church's broader family ministry.

### Duties of a Family-Ministry Committee

- Prays for families in the church and community
- Formulates a mission statement for presentation to and approval by the congregation
- Formulates purpose statements for family ministry in the church and community, based on God's revelation
- Formulates goals and objectives for family ministry, based on a written mission statement
- Articulates the church's philosophy of family ministry
- Assesses the needs of the congregation and the community in regard to family life
- Develops a comprehensive plan for meeting the needs of families
- Leads in the development of a Covenant Marriage policy for church approval and implementation
- Raises the banner for family ministry in all areas of church life
- Encourages and assists church programs in meeting the needs of families
- Conducts special family programs targeted at prevention, enrichment, intervention, and outreach
- Coordinates, stimulates, and promotes the church's family-related ministries through the organization of the church
- Studies social and political issues related to family and informs church members about them[2]

### Qualifications of Family-Ministry Committee Members

- Should sense an invitation by God to serve in this area of ministry
- Should be representative of the families in the congregation (men, women, young, old, single, married, and so forth)
- Should have a burden and vision for family ministry and, if possible, gifts or expertise in this area
- Should not already be overly involved in week-to-week activities in other church ministries[3]

# Ways to Organize
# Your Family Ministry

## Basic Family-Ministry Organization

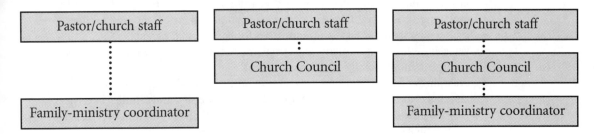

## Expanded Family-Ministry Organization

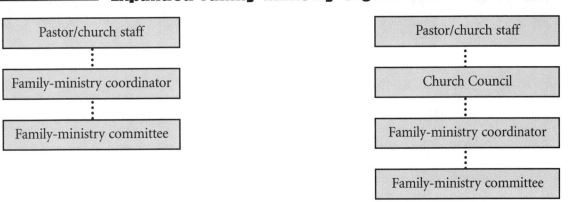

### Job Description for a Family-Ministry Staff Position

Some churches may be able to provide a full-time staff position to support family ministry in their church and community. This position should fall under the guidelines for ministerial employment established by the church's constitution. This minister should be recommended by the senior pastor and should be directly responsible to the senior pastor. Because each church is unique, it should seek God's guidance in developing a job description that reflects your church's heart and call to family ministry. Such a job description should also be comparable in responsibility to the other staff job descriptions in your church. The following job description suggests areas of responsibility and qualifications this position might include.

1. The family minister should be responsible for the care and spiritual development of his or her own family through a system of accountability with the senior pastor, personnel committee, or another designated group.

2. The family minister should be responsible in consultation with the senior pastor for the spiritual direction of all programs, events, and ministries falling under the care of family ministry. This person is responsible for leading the church in discerning God's activity in the families of the church and community and for responding to the needs of couples, parents, and their children in obedience to His call. The family ministry should include but not be limited to the following responsibilities.

Chapter 5: A Form for Family Ministry

- Assessing the needs of families, with an emphasis on marriage and parenting
- Leading the church in the development and implementation of a church-developed-and-approved marriage policy
- Developing and implementing preventative ministries in the lives of individuals, couples, and their families prior to transitional times in their lives
- Overseeing premarital counseling and/or marriage-preparation classes for couples desiring to be married in the church or by a minister on the staff
- Developing and implementing enrichment ministries designed to enhance family life and strengthen relationships with God and family members
- Developing various training-and-enrichment programs for parents and families
- Developing ongoing discipleship ministries for couples and parents
- Overseeing the development and implementation of a biannual marriage-enrichment and/or family-enrichment retreat
- Developing and implementing intervention ministries designed to provide immediate, short- to medium-term care for individuals, couples, and families in crisis
- Overseeing the development of a lay-led ministry of intervention for couples, parents, and their children for immediate, short-term care
- Overseeing the development of support-group ministries for couples and/or families in crisis or those going through life transitions
- Overseeing the development and maintenance of a referral list of Christian counselors in the community for those in need of extended/extensive intervention
- Working with the benevolence ministry in meeting the physical needs of families in the church and community
- Developing and implementing outreach ministries designed to provide opportunities for families to discover and live God's call on their lives as individuals, couples, parents, and families in their communities
- Overseeing the development of a mentoring ministry to newlywed couples
- Working with the benevolence ministry to provide opportunities for family members to minister together
- Working with the missions pastor or missions coordinator to provide opportunities for short-term mission trips for couples and families
- Cooperating with the minister responsible for all areas of ministry to ensure the strength of the church through strengthening and maintaining families' health
- Cooperating with the single-adult minister in the development and administration of single-parent-family ministries.
- Providing counseling and pastoral care for couples, families, parents, and children
- Performing weddings, funerals, and baptisms as called on
3. The family minister should be responsible for the supervision and administration of all family-ministry staff, including evaluations and recommendations, professional development, coordination of ministry plans, and staffing of all programs assigned to family ministry.
4. The family minister should be responsible for the coordination and administration of the family-ministry calendar and budget.
5. The family minister should be a participating member of the pastoral staff, with responsibility for weekly pastoral staff meetings, council meetings, and staff retreats.

---

[1]John W. Drakeford and Claude V. King, *WiseCounsel: Skills for Lay Counseling* (Nashville: LifeWay, 1988), 39–40.
[2]Gary Hauk, *Family Enrichment in Your Church* (Nashville: Convention, 1988), 73.
[3]Charles M. Sell, *Family Ministry* (Grand Rapids: Zondervan, 1995), 349–51.

# The Leaders of Family Ministry

# Chapter 6

People volunteer to serve for a variety of reasons. These reasons vary in degrees of sincerity and many times come from wrong motives. To develop effective family ministry requires effective leadership. How can leaders be found for family ministry? Praying for the discernment of the Holy Spirit is essential as you search for leaders.

## Qualities of a Leader

As you seek God's will in providing effective family-ministry leaders, you should look for certain qualities. These are not qualifications for leadership but character qualities to identify and nurture in those God is calling to minister with you.

> **Praying for the discernment of the Holy Spirit is essential as you search for leaders**

*Growing.* Family-ministry leaders should be growing in their personal walks with God. God will prepare those He wants to bring alongside you in ministry, and He will do this through a personal, growing love relationship with Him.

*Available.* Family-ministry leaders allow God to direct their time and priorities to serve Him and are open to meeting family needs.

*Encouraging.* Family-ministry leaders can encourage others God has brought alongside them as recipients of the ministry or as colaborers in the ministry.

*Serving.* Family-ministry leaders have a passion for serving the Lord by ministering to families.

*Caring.* Family-ministry leaders care about the issues families face in our society, and they have a burden for the lost.

*Transparent.* Family-ministry leaders admit their own failures and weaknesses so that those God brings alongside them will be able to approach them when struggling.

*Nurturing/discipling.* Family-ministry leaders are as concerned about team members' spiritual growth as they are about training them to lead others.

*Listening.* Family-ministry leaders know how to listen to those they are leading so that they understand their hearts. Believing that God speaks through fellow believers, they affirm team members' contributions as important.

*Flexible.* Family-ministry leaders know how to adjust their lives to join God where He is working.

*Dependable.* Family-ministry leaders stand by their convictions and commitments, trusting that the Holy Spirit will strengthen them for the task.

*Accountable.* Family-ministry leaders allow and expect the Lord and the team to hold them accountable for their leadership and spiritual walks.

*Willing to delegate.* Family-ministry leaders relinquish control of the ministry and allow others to take responsibilities without watching over each detail. They allow others the freedom to be creative.

*Training by example.* Family-ministry leaders continue to learn so that they can train others and keep them informed of available training opportunities.

*Able to evaluate.* Family-ministry leaders evaluate activities, studies, leaders, and ministries to make sure they are effective and current.

*Innovative.* Family-ministry leaders are able to see where God is working and join Him. They are not afraid to step out of their comfort zones if God leads them to do so. They are not afraid of the statement "We've never done it that way before."

Is leadership something that is designated, taught, acquired, or accomplished? Leaders arrive in their positions through all of these methods. However, the position does not make the leader. Leadership is a gift from God. It is the ability to influence others to move toward a common goal or invest their lives in a common cause. In family ministry it is leading God's people to join Him in ministering to the needs of families.

The leadership style necessary to minister to the needs of families is one of servanthood. In Matthew 20:25-28 Jesus called His disciples together and clearly set forth the criterion for leadership that glorifies the Father. Jesus stated: " 'You know that the rulers of the Gentiles lord it over them, and those who are great exercise authority over them. Yet it shall not be so among you; but whoever desires to become great among you, let him be your servant. And whoever desires to be first among you, let him be your slave—just as the Son of Man did not come to be served, but to serve, and to give His life a ransom for many' " (NKJV). You are not looking for those who desire to rule over others. You are looking for those who are willing to serve others.

## Recruiting Leaders

Often our methods of recruiting leaders for church positions are borrowed from the world. We may seek leaders with a predetermined notion in mind: we want natural leaders with great talents, a wonderful imagination, charisma, and tremendous energy who can take charge. Of course, such persons come along, but God chooses the ordinary to accomplish the extraordinary. There are many in whom God has placed a burden for family ministry and through whom God can accomplish His work beyond our expectations.

> **God chooses the ordinary to accomplish the extraordinary**

When the apostles met in an upper room after Jesus' crucifixion, they prayed for guidance in selecting a replacement for Judas. When the seven were chosen for ministry to the widows in Acts 6, the church knew the duties they needed these men to perform. In modern terms the apostles proposed a job description that was then approved by the congregation. The church also knew the characteristics that were required to carry out the responsibilities. With these in mind, seven men were chosen.

Likewise, you first need to pray for guidance in selecting the individuals God wants to use in the area of family ministry. Determine what the leadership needs are and pray for God to provide the right leaders to fulfill those responsibilities. Watch and see whom God sends to join you in ministering to the needs of families.

Based on the goals and objectives you have identified for family ministry, what type of leaders will you need to carry out the various ministries? For example, if one of your goals is to provide marriage-enrichment events, what type of leaders would be needed?

Sometimes it is easy to spot persons who have natural interests in serving families. Someone may express concern about activities for families, senior adults, or couples. Even though such persons may not appear to be leaders at first glance, God may be preparing them to assume leadership responsibilities.

You may discover family-ministry leaders by identifying persons who are already addressing family issues in your church. Some leaders, such as adult Bible-study teachers, discipleship-training leaders, senior-adult workers, and youth leaders, have jobs that include responsibilities to minister to families. These and others may already provide family ministry in an informal way. They may be keenly interested in family ministry and may be particularly gifted for it, just waiting for you to recruit them formally.

## Training Leaders

It is important to train family-ministry leaders. You can use this resource as a tool for training all who commit to serve on the family-ministry committee. Plan six 60-minute training sessions for praying; processing information; developing a mission statement, goals, and objectives; and sharing ideas. Prior to each session ask each person to read

the corresponding chapter or chapters in this book. Consider the following schedule.
- Session 1: Chapter 1
- Session 2: Chapters 2–3
- Session 3: Chapter 4
- Session 4: Chapters 5–6
- Session 5: Chapter 7
- Session 6: Chapters 8–9

All persons who accept leadership positions for events, projects, or courses could benefit from reading this resource to learn your basic strategy for ministry. If those you approach know that they will receive training in the area in which you are asking them to serve, they will be more willing to accept.

Others may have backgrounds in leadership, but without training they may lead in a direction other than the one you have in mind. In any ministry certain ongoing training is required. Ongoing training recognizes the importance of the task you are asking your leaders to do. LifeWay Christian Resources has developed a wide range of training materials for leaders. Christian Growth Study Plan diplomas are available in any area for which you might wish to train and recognize your leaders. Ask your church's minister of education for information. Be sure to request Christian Growth Study Plan credit for leaders who complete this book. Directions for requesting credit may be found on page 64.

> **Ongoing training recognizes the importance of the task**

Consider discipleship training as an opportunity to train your leaders. What about leadership training through the association or state convention? One very effective way to train your leaders, as well as provide time for planning and strengthening relationships, is to attend a national Discipleship and Family Week at LifeWay Ridgecrest Conference Center in Ridgecrest, North Carolina, or LifeWay Glorieta Conference Center in Glorieta, New Mexico.[1] Whatever form of training you provide, publicly recognizing leaders when they complete their training will give them confidence and will increase the credibility of the ministry. Consider recognizing leaders' training accomplishments during a worship service, through the church newsletter, or at a special event.

John Maxwell has said, "Never do ministry alone."[2] The best resource for training is you! The most dedicated leaders come through mentoring. Training by example is one of the most effective ways to develop leadership for the next generation.

## Maintaining Leaders

Is it important to feel appreciated? Certainly it is. One of the best ways to maintain your leaders is to let them know that they are appreciated. Give encouragement and compliments. A formal recognition on an annual basis before the church or before the leader's particular ministry group is a great morale booster.

*The Five Love Languages* by Gary Chapman teaches that each of us sends and receives messages of love and appreciation from one of five primary emotional love languages. These languages are gifts, quality time, physical touch, words of affirmation, and acts of service. Therefore, you need to be sensitive to the various languages your leaders speak so that your expressions of affirmation are communicated in ways they appreciate. Not all leaders appreciate a gift or public verbal affirmation. One of the best things you can do is to discover each leader's love language and seek to affirm him or her in the language that communicates best with that leader.

---

[1]For information write to Family Ministry; LifeWay Christian Resources; 127 Ninth Avenue, North; Nashville, TN 37234.
[2]John Maxwell, speech at lay-ministry conference; First Baptist Church; Springdale, AR; 26 August 1995.

# Chapter 7

# Tools for Planning Family Ministry

As you consider the tools available to help you carry out family ministry, remember that you are joining the Master in His work. Family ministry is His ministry, and all of His resources are available to you, including spiritual resources, people resources, time resources, financial resources, and printed resources. God is the source of all the resources you need to minister to families.

## Family Demographics

One way to obtain information about families in your church and community is through the Census Bureau. Census information provides you basic information on the family structures in your church and community. If you are a Southern Baptist, you can obtain demographic information for your ZIP-code area from the North American Mission Board; 4200 North Point Parkway; Alpharetta, GA 30022-4174; (770) 410-6000. This information is vital to the development of family ministry, providing you an idea of the number of family units in your church or community; couples with and without children; parents of preschoolers, elementary-age children, teenagers, and college students; remarried couples and blended families; older families; single parents; and engaged or newlywed couples. This kind of information can help you identify what God has already done and can help you begin assessing where He wants you to join Him in the future. You may also want to ask questions about education, income, longevity of residence, distance from church, occupation, or special skills and talents. However, don't ask questions you don't need.

> **God is the source of all the resources you need to minister to families**

## Family Growth Needs

The tool on the following page can be used to grasp needs generally taking place in families at different stages in the family life cycle. As you read column 2, underline any needs you think stand out in your congregation or community. Respond in column 3. By looking at family growth needs, you may be led to join God in addressing a particular concern. For example, in looking at the stage of early parenting, you may get in touch with spiritual/moral development needs for children. This may lead you to provide a parenting seminar in your church or community, using *Shaping the Next Generation* (see "Ministry Resources," beginning on p. 57).

## Family Needs Forum

Another vital tool for listening to God speak through His people is a Family Needs Forum, which is a focused time to identify and prioritize family needs to which your church may minister. The Family Needs Forum brings together interested church members, usually youth through adults, for an evening of small-group activities. The group divides into teams, which brainstorm family needs, prioritize them, and plan suggested strategies to meet those needs.

Be aware that this process depends on the principle of laypersons' involvement in developing ideas and contributing leadership. Participants can be expected to come out of the forum highly motivated and ready to accept the primary responsibility for family ministry. Utilize the people you discover. An effort by the church staff to dominate this process will detract from this motivation and sense of responsibility.

# Family Growth Needs

| Stage in Family Life Cycle | Education/Enrichment/Ministry Needs | Is This a Need in Your Church? | Community? |
|---|---|---|---|
| **Premarriage and early marriage** | Understanding marriage and realistic expectations; communication skills; money management; sexual adjustment; birth intentions; decision making; conflict management; relationship with extended family; personal and spiritual growth | ❏ Yes ❏ No | ❏ Yes ❏ No |
| **Early parenting** | Child development; discipline; development of children's self-esteem; spiritual and moral development of children; emotional and spiritual climate of home; self-esteem of parents; strengthening marriage | ❏ Yes ❏ No | ❏ Yes ❏ No |
| **Parenting adolescents** | Physical, emotional, and spiritual needs of teens; parental role in preparation for career and for marriage or single life; strengthening marriage | ❏ Yes ❏ No | ❏ Yes ❏ No |
| **Empty nest** | Strengthening marriage; helping children grow toward independence; relationship with aging parents; retirement preparation | ❏ Yes ❏ No | ❏ Yes ❏ No |
| **Retirement** | Significant relationships; self-esteem; service in church and community; autonomy; money management; relationship with children, grandchildren, and great-grandchildren; physical and mental health; maintaining home if health fails; acceptance of death of spouse and peers; facing death | ❏ Yes ❏ No | ❏ Yes ❏ No |

| Special Circumstances in Some Families | Education/Enrichment/Ministry Needs | Is This a Need in Your Church? | Community? |
|---|---|---|---|
| **Refilled nest** | Relationship with grown children or grandchildren who move back home; strengthening marriage | ❏ Yes ❏ No | ❏ Yes ❏ No |
| **Single parents** | Grief process; helping children adjust; intimacy needs of parents; adjustments to demands of household management, earning living, and rearing children alone or loss of children by noncustodial parent; relationship with extended family; lack of acceptance of divorced persons by church; spiritual growth | ❏ Yes ❏ No | ❏ Yes ❏ No |
| **Blended families** | Marriage adjustment; adjustment of children to stepparents and stepsiblings; relationship with former spouses and extended families; blending lifestyles; spiritual growth | ❏ Yes ❏ No | ❏ Yes ❏ No |
| **Childless families** | Strengthening marriage; personal and spiritual growth; dealing with infertility; choice to be childless; adjustment to childlessness; relationship with extended family; career adjustments | ❏ Yes ❏ No | ❏ Yes ❏ No |
| **Intercultural** | Marriage adjustments; insight on cultural differences in family expectations; child rearing; spiritual growth; establishing family culture and creating family uniqueness through blending cultures | ❏ Yes ❏ No | ❏ Yes ❏ No |
| **Interfaith** | Identifying differences in belief systems; communication skills; assessing impact of family of origin; spiritual growth as a couple; development of unified personal family faith system; growth in personal relationship with the Lord | ❏ Yes ❏ No | ❏ Yes ❏ No |
| **Grandparents rearing grandchildren** | Adjustment to full-time children; awareness of grief factors; anger; information on child rearing; legal issues; lifestyle changes; support ministries; child-care relief | ❏ Yes ❏ No | ❏ Yes ❏ No |

The Family Needs Forum should be held in a large room with plenty of front-wall space for hanging large sheets of paper or for projecting transparencies. Have available pencils and paper for every person. Also have large sheets of paper (24 by 30 inches), felt-tip markers, and tape or an overhead projector.

1. Begin with a brief three- to four-minute devotional about meeting family needs. Consider using Galatians 6:2.

**Participants come out of the forum highly motivated**

2. Divide into teams of six to eight members, separating family members and mixing youth with adults. Each team is to appoint a scribe and spokesperson. Provide a sheet of paper and one pencil for each person.

3. Ask each person to think of a family he or she knows in the church and to list on a sheet of paper three needs of this family. Tell members not to identify the families they consider. If they draw a blank, ask them to write down their responses to this question: What needs do you see in the families of this church?

4. When all have finished, have everyone fold the sheet once and place it in a stack. Then have teams exchange stacks once and then again with a different team until the stacks are no longer identifiable. When exchanges are completed, each team is to distribute the sheets among its members. Some individuals may have two sheets.

5. Each team is to compile one team list of needs. Each person offers one item, going around the group. The others are to omit items that have already been mentioned. Continue until all items have been covered by a statement or phrase on the team list. The scribe in each team records.

6. When each team has compiled one list, reconvene the entire group. Call for one or two scribes to print each statement on large sheets of paper or on overhead cels. The presiding leader compiles the information from each team in a round-robin inquiry. Each team calls out only one item while the other teams edit and delete items already mentioned. Continue around the room from one group to another until all of the unduplicated needs mentioned have been written on the large sheets of paper or on overhead cels.

7. Ask teams to prioritize the items on the master list. Give each team a total of six votes. Three votes will be cast for the item it considers to be top priority, two votes for its second highest priority, and one vote for its third highest priority. The decisions about priority are to be discussed in the team until all members agree.

8. Receive the votes from each team one at a time and record them by making hash marks above each item on the master list with different colors of felt-tip markers. On a separate large sheet of paper or an overhead cel, relist the items receiving votes in order of priority. Number the items.

9. (Delete steps 9 and 10 if time is short.) Assign each team the final task of brainstorming actions the church might take to meet the top five needs listed by the group. Say: Brainstorm and list on one sheet of paper your ideas about possible actions this church could take to meet the top five needs. All ideas will be accepted.

10. Display five large sheets of paper or five overhead cels with one of the five top priority items printed at the top of each. Receive the ideas in the same fashion you recorded needs.

11. Review the purposes of the Family Needs Forum. Indicate that this information will be used to help your church meet real family needs. Share your dream for family ministry and your plans for the next few weeks. Ask each person to take a sheet of paper and record the following information: their impression of the event; whether they would be willing to help lead the church to meet these needs; and their name, address, and phone number if they expressed a willingness to help.

12. Collect everyone's paper. Have a closing devotional and a prayer of dedication for the launch of this ministry.[1]

# Needs and Interests Survey

This reproducible tool provides you an opportunity to learn the total church family's needs and interests. Many surveys in churches are never used. Many have never been completed or have little significance. Often, previously conducted surveys are used, so that the church bases its ministries on outdated information. This survey will help you assess where God wants you to join Him in ministering to the families in your church and community.

The following survey can be done at church or through organized home visits. If it is done at church, it should be done when you can involve most families. After taking the survey, use "Needs and Interests Survey Planning Sheet" (see p. 47) to compile the information that was shared. Then include this information in the total family-ministry picture.

> **This survey will help you assess where God wants you to join Him**

## Needs and Interests Survey

Please take a few moments to fill out this survey of personal interests, needs, and concerns so that we, as a church, can plan more effective ministries for you as individuals, couples, parents, and grandparents.

You are important to our church. This survey will be used to help us establish future priorities, goals, and directions for ministry. As a church, we want to help you experience God's love at home and at church.

## General Information About You

Check all that apply.

Age:
- ❏ 13–17
- ❏ 18–25
- ❏ 26–34
- ❏ 35–55
- ❏ 56–65
- ❏ 66–74
- ❏ 75–79
- ❏ 80–89
- ❏ 90+

Gender: ❏ Male ❏ Female

Status:
- ❏ Single, never married
- ❏ Single, divorced/separated
- ❏ Single, widow/widower
- ❏ Married
- ❏ Married again
- ❏ Parent, traditional family
- ❏ Parent, single family
- ❏ Parent, blended family
- ❏ Custodial
- ❏ Noncustodial
- ❏ Joint custody
- ❏ Foster parent

Employment:
- ❏ Full-time homemaker
- ❏ Full-time outside the home
- ❏ Unemployed
- ❏ Home-based business
- ❏ Part-time outside the home
- ❏ Retired

Ages of children at home: _____

## Areas of Need/Interest

Check all applicable topics you would be willing to participate in or lead.

I prefer groups for ❏ Women only ❏ Men only ❏ General audiences
❏ Couples ❏ Peers only

### Personal

| Participate in: | Lead: | Participate in: | Lead: |
|---|---|---|---|
| ❏ Spiritual life | ❏ | ❏ Dealing with anger | ❏ |
| ❏ Caring for aging parents | ❏ | ❏ Calligraphy | ❏ |
| ❏ Conflict resolution | ❏ | ❏ Cooking/nutrition | ❏ |
| ❏ Dealing with crises | ❏ | ❏ Creative writing | ❏ |
| ❏ Drama | ❏ | ❏ Exercise | ❏ |

| Participate in: | Lead: | Participate in: | Lead: |
|---|---|---|---|
| ❑ Financial planning | ❑ | ❑ First aid (with CPR) | ❑ |
| ❑ Gardening | ❑ | ❑ Home repair | ❑ |
| ❑ Car repair | ❑ | ❑ Interior decorating | ❑ |
| ❑ Marriage enrichment | ❑ | ❑ Needlework | ❑ |
| ❑ Quilting | ❑ | ❑ Sewing | ❑ |
| ❑ Painting | ❑ | ❑ Ceramics | ❑ |
| ❑ Parenting | ❑ | ❑ Personal grooming | ❑ |
| ❑ Safety and self-defense | ❑ | ❑ Grief recovery | ❑ |
| ❑ Time management | ❑ | ❑ Divorce recovery | ❑ |
| ❑ Finding a job | ❑ | ❑ Job security | ❑ |
| ❑ Balancing job, family, ministry | ❑ | ❑ Basic budgeting | ❑ |
| ❑ Other: _____ | ❑ | ❑ Other: _____ | ❑ |

## Married Couples

Check all topics you need or would like to study.

- ❑ Being a Christian husband
- ❑ Being a Christian wife
- ❑ Biblical perspective of marriage
- ❑ Dealing with in-laws
- ❑ Equality and submission in marriage
- ❑ Growing in oneness
- ❑ Husband/wife communication
- ❑ Intimacy in marriage
- ❑ Listening to my mate
- ❑ Mentoring
- ❑ Newlywed adjustment
- ❑ Sexual fulfillment in marriage
- ❑ Two-career marriage
- ❑ Other: _____

## Parenting

Check all topics you need or would like to study.

- ❑ Being a Christian father
- ❑ Being a Christian mother
- ❑ Communicating moral values
- ❑ Dealing with hectic schedules
- ❑ Discipline
- ❑ Helping children after divorce
- ❑ How to teach children about sex
- ❑ Parenting college students
- ❑ Leading your children to Christ
- ❑ Finances
- ❑ Parenting exceptional/special children
- ❑ Parenting preschoolers
- ❑ Parenting 6- to 12-year-olds
- ❑ Parenting teens
- ❑ Parenting in the blended family
- ❑ Single parenting
- ❑ Career planning/changes
- ❑ Stress/burnout
- ❑ Other: _____

## Youth

Check all topics you need or would like to study.

- ❑ Dating
- ❑ Discovering God's will
- ❑ Facing issues at school
- ❑ Getting along with siblings
- ❑ Getting along with peers
- ❑ Sexual abstinence
- ❑ Getting along with parents
- ❑ Getting ready for marriage/family
- ❑ Improving self-esteem
- ❑ Making right moral decisions
- ❑ Preparing for a career
- ❑ Other: _____

## General Family

Check all topics you need or would like to study.

- ❑ Becoming a healthy family
- ❑ Understanding blended-family dynamics
- ❑ Improving family communication
- ❑ Starting family worship and Bible study
- ❑ Adjusting to being a single-parent family
- ❑ Building family traditions
- ❑ Finding God's will as a family
- ❑ Providing family recreation
- ❑ Developing healthful eating habits

## Single Adults

Check all topics you need or would like to study.

- ❑ Experiencing fulfillment
- ❑ Discovering my place in the church
- ❑ Life after college, starting a career
- ❑ Dating
- ❑ Dealing with single-again issues
- ❑ Coping with loneliness
- ❑ Relationships with the opposite sex
- ❑ Developing meaningful friendships
- ❑ Preparing for marriage/remarriage
- ❑ Surviving college
- ❑ Coping with the loss of a mate
- ❑ Other: _____

## Senior Adults

Check all topics you need or would like to study.

- ❑ Caregiving for …
  - ❑ Spouse
  - ❑ Relative
  - ❑ Child
  - ❑ Grandchild
- ❑ Dealing with loss
  - ❑ Health
  - ❑ Spouse
  - ❑ Independence
  - ❑ Job
- ❑ Family issues
- ❑ Grandparenting
- ❑ Spiritual journey
- ❑ Other: _____
- ❑ Marital issues
- ❑ Divorce
  - ❑ Separation
  - ❑ Remarriage
  - ❑ Relocation
- ❑ Homes
- ❑ Retirement centers
  - ❑ Assisted-living care
  - ❑ Nursing-home care
- ❑ Retirement issues
- ❑ Prayer life
- ❑ Relating to grown children
- ❑ Volunteer opportunities
- ❑ Other: _____

## Fellowship

I prefer groups for     ❑ Women only     ❑ Men only     ❑ General audiences
                        ❑ Couples        ❑ Peers only

- ❑ Retreats (Friday night and Saturday)
- ❑ Conferences at church
- ❑ After-church fellowship
- ❑ Dinner clubs
- ❑ Prayer/share partners
- ❑ New-member activities
- ❑ Banquets and luncheons
- ❑ Other: _____

## Study Opportunities

I prefer groups for     ❑ Women only     ❑ Men only     ❑ General audiences
                        ❑ Couples        ❑ Peers only

- ❑ Discipleship studies
- ❑ Identifying spiritual gifts for ministry
- ❑ Bible study:     ❑ Weekday          ❑ Weekday noon
                     ❑ Weekday evening  ❑ Sunday evening
- ❑ Book reviews (type: _____)
- ❑ Study of social and moral issues in our society
- ❑ Study of how to help others with personal problems
- ❑ Other: _____

## Missions and Evangelism

I prefer groups for  ❑ Women only  ❑ Men only  ❑ General audiences
                      ❑ Couples  ❑ Peers only

❑ Witness training          ❑ Praying for missionaries
❑ Missions studies          ❑ Interaction with local missionaries
❑ Short-term mission trip:  ❑ USA          ❑ Overseas
❑ Other: _____

## Community Ministries

If you speak a second language, please specify: _____
I would be willing to help our church expand its ministry in ...

❑ Literacy                              ❑ Clothes closet
❑ Tutoring                              ❑ Meals on wheels
❑ Children's home                       ❑ Latchkey kids/hotline
❑ Prisons/jails/youth offenders         ❑ Internationals
❑ Campus ministry                       ❑ Hospital ministry
❑ Handicapped/disabled persons          ❑ Homebound
❑ Nursing homes/adopted grandparents/aging  ❑ Medical/dentistry
❑ Soup kitchen                          ❑ Other: _____

## Teaching/Leading

Check the areas you would like to teach or lead and the age group you prefer
to work with.

|                              | Preschoolers | Children | Youth | Adults |
|------------------------------|:------------:|:--------:|:-----:|:------:|
| ❑ Bible studies              | ❑ | ❑ | ❑ | ❑ |
| ❑ Music                      | ❑ | ❑ | ❑ | ❑ |
| ❑ Vacation Bible School      | ❑ | ❑ | ❑ | ❑ |
| ❑ Retreats/conferences       | ❑ | ❑ | ❑ | ❑ |
| ❑ Camps                      | ❑ | ❑ | ❑ | ❑ |
| ❑ Discipleship studies       | ❑ | ❑ | ❑ | ❑ |
| ❑ Intercessory prayer ministry | ❑ | ❑ | ❑ | ❑ |
| ❑ Accountability groups      | ❑ | ❑ | ❑ | ❑ |
| ❑ Special-interest studies   | ❑ | ❑ | ❑ | ❑ |

## Service

I would be willing to serve my church through ...

❑ Artwork                       ❑ Newsletters
❑ Bulletin boards               ❑ Photography
❑ Creative displays             ❑ Posters
❑ Creative writing              ❑ Telephoning
❑ Distribution of information   ❑ Book reviews
❑ Graphics                      ❑ Nursery volunteers
❑ Music                         ❑ Your specialty: _____

Thank you for sharing this information with us.

Name: _____

Address: _____

Phone: _____ (home) _____(work)

# Needs and Interests Survey Planning Sheet

Use the following information to develop a planning sheet for a comprehensive ministry that builds strong families in your church and community.

1. Compile the information gathered from "Needs and Interests Survey." What is God saying to you through the church about ministering to families?
2. In each area checked on the survey, identify the specific type(s) of need found among persons in your church and community.
3. Identify the distinctive need(s). Because the needs listed do not include all needs, you may want to identify others. The information you receive may be overwhelming. Determine where God wants you to join Him and address those needs.
4. Prioritize the needs. Select and list the distinctive needs that God reveals as priorities for your church. Include these as you continue to listen to God speak through His church. Remember that every need can't be met through your ministry, nor can all needs be met at once.
5. With these priorities, set and list goals for your ministry. Complete this sentence for each priority: With this priority we want to work toward _____ this year.
6. Determine and list actions to reach your goals. What events, projects, or programs will you choose? Use this book as a planning tool.

---

[1]Gary Hauk, *Family Enrichment in Your Church* (Nashville: Convention, 1988), 41–44.

# Chapter 8

# Tools for Implementing Family Ministry

After you have discovered the needs of the families in your church and community, you must provide ministry opportunities to meet those needs. You must also develop strategies for raising the congregation's awareness of these needs. You can select from several tools to provide an intentional, comprehensive ministry to families. Here are some possibilities to consider.

## Christian Home Emphasis

Christian Home Emphasis sets aside a block of time on the church calendar to focus on the needs of families. Beginning the week prior to Mother's Day and continuing through Father's Day, this emphasis offers you a great opportunity to provide activities and studies for all ages through discipleship-training courses. It calls churches to intentionally focus on the families God has brought into their fellowship. Christian Home Emphasis provides an opportunity to join God in ministering to the various family needs in your church body. This section provides background content for you to use in sharing the heart of Christian Home Emphasis.

The theme of Christian Home Emphasis 2001 is Building Strong Families Through Complete Surrender. This begins with parents. The strength of the family will not exceed the strength of the primary caregivers in the home.

In Deuteronomy 5 Moses shared with Israel the Ten Commandments given by the Lord their God. Having initiated a covenant with His people at Horeb, God then gave them laws for their protection and provision. Their response was " 'We will listen and obey' " (Deut. 5:27, NIV). The Lord's response was " 'I have heard what this people said to you. Everything they said was good. Oh, that their hearts would be inclined to fear me and keep all my commands always, so that it might go well with them and their children forever' " (Deut. 5:28-29, NIV). Their obligation was to obey the laws of the covenant that God had given them.

> **The strength of the family will not exceed the strength of the primary caregivers**

In Deuteronomy 6 Moses set forth the reason for these laws: " 'So that you, your children and their children after them may fear the Lord your God … and so that you may enjoy long life. Hear, O Israel, and be careful to obey so that it may go well with you and that you may increase greatly in a land flowing with milk and honey, just as the Lord, the God of your fathers, promised you' " (Deut. 6:2-3, NIV). Then Moses explained the pattern God's people should follow to fulfill their responsibility of the covenant relationship. They were to " 'love the Lord your God with all your heart and with all your soul and with all your strength. These commandments that I give you today are to be upon your hearts' " (Deut. 6:4-5, NIV).

Where do we begin building strong families? We begin with our obedience to the Lord, who has initiated a covenant of love with us. Each of us is to love Him with all our heart and with all our soul and with all our strength. Parents have been given the awesome responsibility of joining God's act of creating and developing His children. To join God in this activity, we must go back to basics.

To build strong families, we must live in a covenant relationship with God:
• One that supersedes all other relationships
• One that is marked by complete surrender to His will

• One that demonstrates complete obedience to His commandments of love

Then and only then can we begin to impress these laws and this covenant relationship on our children. When we do, we will experience the joy of establishing and maintaining a strong family that will grow in Christ from generation to generation. We must incline our hearts to fear God and keep all His commands always, so that it might go well with us and our children forever. That is the promise given to us by the giver of the covenant. God alone initiates such a covenant, and God is the only one who can bring it to pass. Our role is to hear His Word and obey.

## The Covenant Marriage Movement

For the past 30 years we as a nation have wandered in the wilderness of "no-fault" divorce. Too often, the church, as the bride of Christ, has sacrificed the truth about marriage as God intended on the altar of tolerance. We have chosen to remain silent in the face of blatantly self-centered divorce, fearing that we would offend those who have experienced it. We have relegated hundreds of thousands of couples to a fate of silent suffering because we didn't want to be perceived as interfering. We have maintained that we believe marriage should last a lifetime, while doing little or nothing to help ensure that it does.

Today God is calling couples back to a righteous relationship with Him and to one another in marriage. Couples are becoming more and more aware of the need to take seriously the vows they made on their wedding day. They want their love to last for a lifetime. The Covenant Marriage Movement is a movement of God in the hearts and lives of couples and among churches, denominations, ministries, and organizations to come together and share God's message about marriage with one voice.

> **God is calling couples back to a righteous relationship with Him**

### The Congregation's Responsibility

A Covenant Marriage congregation is one that commits to provide a ministry to married couples who are members of their congregation or who are planning to be married within their congregation based on the following statement of affirmation.

> Believing that marriage is a covenant intended by God to be a lifelong, fruitful relationship between a man and a woman, we vow to God, each other, our family, and our community to remain steadfast in unconditional love, reconciliation, and sexual purity, while purposefully growing in our covenant-marriage relationship.

When a married couple unites with a congregation, the congregation enters a covenant relationship with that couple and their family. That covenant, initiated by God, is lived through the local body of Christ. The congregation, as the bride of Christ, is one of God's expressions of His unconditional love for that couple. Therefore, each local congregation, in obedience to the covenant given to them by God, has the responsibility to unconditionally love that couple as Christ loves the church and gave Himself for it. We as God's people are not only to be keepers of the covenant but also to be participants in it as well.

When a couple comes to your church to be united in holy matrimony, the congregation is responsible for helping them examine their hearts to confirm and affirm what God desires for them in this union. Just as it is important for us to examine our hearts before partaking in holy communion, which symbolizes our affirmation of God's gift of His covenant love, we must also examine our hearts before entering a covenant of marriage. Therefore, each couple who is to be married in your congregation needs to spend time in premarital preparation. This preparation focuses on God's gift of marriage; the centrality of God in the home; and the couple's responsibility to be obedient to God, the giver of the covenant.

Marriage preparation should include elements such as—
- a study of Scripture related to marriage and the covenant;
- administration of a personality inventory;
- at least six sessions with an approved marriage-preparation couple or a minister of the congregation;
- a commitment to unite with a newly married or young married-couples class whose focus is on enriching or enhancing God's gift of marriage.

When a couple stands before the altar of a local congregation, not only are the man and the woman entering a covenant together with God, but we as a congregation are entering a covenant with that couple. Our presence at that union, through our clergy and/or congregation, affirms what we know to be God's desire to unite the man and the woman as husband and wife. The congregation, therefore, makes a covenant with the couple to love them unconditionally and nurture them in a growing love relationship through the fellowship of the church.

We recommend that Covenant Marriage congregations offer the following ministries for couples. We realize that not all congregations are alike, nor do they have the same resources. You may be the only staff person in your congregation. But we also realize that some of the most valuable time you spend in ministry is spent with couples preparing for and living in a covenant-marriage relationship.

1. The first and most difficult step is to establish and affirm a Covenant Marriage Policy as a congregation. This policy must be the work of the congregation in order to remain in effect when church-staff members come and go. It also provides guidelines and support to staff members who are being pressured by well-meaning parents or overzealous couples. This marriage policy goes much deeper than facility management and fee structure. The policy must focus on the couple, their relationship with God and each other, and the congregation's commitment to their marriage. The congregation should value the marriage more than the wedding. A wedding is for a day, but a marriage is for a lifetime. Therefore, your congregation's Covenant Marriage Policy must include marriage preparation. When a couple comes to set a date and reserve the church for their wedding, this is the time to join God's activity in their lives through prayer. Someone in the church needs to begin praying for that couple as they begin the marriage-preparation period and enter a covenant marriage. Provide at least six marriage-preparation sessions, in addition to the ceremony planning, and two additional sessions during the first year of marriage. We encourage you to use a marriage-preparation inventory during some of these sessions to help couples communicate specific concerns that may arise.

> A wedding is for a day, but a marriage is for a lifetime

2. Provide a sermon series of at least four messages on relationships, marriage, and/or family. These messages should focus on biblical teachings on establishing and enhancing relationships, the value of covenant-marriage relationships, building strong families, and growing as Christian families in ministry and missions.

3. Provide resources such as books, magazines, tapes, videos, and interactive courses to undergird and strengthen covenant marriages. These could be checked out or purchased by couples.

4. Provide at least one annual marriage-enrichment retreat. This overnight experience for couples should focus on relationship enhancement, skill development, and spiritual refreshment. The format should include instruction, couple activities, and group interaction.

5. Provide at least one annual Covenant Marriage service during which couples in your congregation are offered an opportunity to reaffirm their marriage vows. Covenant Marriage Celebration Sunday will be launched the third Sunday of February 2002. Offer couples an opportunity to sign the Covenant Marriage Couple's Commitment Card provided through the national Covenant Marriage office at (800) 268-1343 or at *www.covenantmarriage.com.*

6. Provide an ongoing prayer ministry for the nearly/newly married. Enlist individuals and couples to pray once a week for each couple for one year. The couple can share specific needs with their prayer couple. If appropriate, the couples can meet together for fellowship and prayer once a quarter.

7. Provide a mentoring ministry for newlywed couples during the first two years of marriage. The mentoring couples should be well founded in their faith and their marriage.

8. Provide ongoing youth studies of at least four sessions on developing healthy relationships, dating, choosing your mate, and marriage. These studies, designed to guide young people to explore these key life decisions from a biblical perspective, could be implemented in a retreat format.

In addition to the actions an individual congregation can take to implement Covenant Marriage, churches of various denominations are pulling together in their respective communities to offer a unified commitment to strengthen marriages and families by offering Covenant Marriage courses (see "Ministry Resources," beginning on p. 57) and by initiating a Community Marriage Policy or a Community Marriage Covenant. You may want to consider initiating a Community Marriage Covenant with other churches in your community.

God is also raising the awareness of state policy makers to the reality that God's original design for marriage and family is the best design. Several states have passed laws that provide couples the option of entering a covenant marriage, which requires marriage preparation and, except for extreme cases, extensive counseling before a divorce can be finalized. By signing the Covenant Marriage Covenant, couples can affirm the importance of a covenant-marriage relationship. But more personally, they can commit or recommit to each other to remain steadfast in the unconditional love God expects of them and provides for them. Find out what your state legislators are doing to strengthen marriages and families. You can help raise the awareness about Covenant Marriage in your community without taking a political stance in support of any particular politician.

God has brought together more than 45 denominations, institutions, and ministries to raise His voice for covenant marriage. This movement is supported by government, community, and educational leaders. The Covenant Marriage Movement is not a human movement but a movement of God. He has placed us in a unique position of joining Him to bring true revival to couples and families in our nation. He has extended an invitation to the cooperating ministries of the Covenant Marriage Movement to join Him, and we have said, "Yes, Lord." He is also inviting local congregations to establish a holistic ministry to married couples that is built on an understanding of marriage as a covenant.

> **The Covenant Marriage Movement is a movement of God**

For more information on topics addressed in this section or on how you can register your congregation as a Covenant Marriage Congregation, call the movement's toll-free number at (800) 268-1343 or visit our Web site at *www.covenantmarriage.com.*

## Building Families Fit 4 Service

Building strong families involves developing good habits for our physical health as well as other areas of our lives. First Corinthians 6:19-20 asks: "Do you not know that your body is a temple of the Holy Spirit, who is in you, whom you have received from God?

You are not your own; you were bought at a price. Therefore honor God with your body" (NIV). Honoring God with our bodies and with those of our families has become a very low priority among church members. Statistics from the National Institutes of Health showed that in 1998, 55 percent of Americans were considered overweight or obese, according to the guidelines of Body Mass Index calculations.[1] The World Health Organization reports that nearly 300,000 people die each year of obesity-related diseases.[2] And while adults are getting heavier, so are children, with a reported 40 percent increase in adolescent obesity in the past decade.[3] These figures are accentuated by the staggering fact that only 1 of 10 persons participates in a regular exercise program.[4] Is practical, user-friendly, biblically based nutrition and exercise information of value to families today? Yes. This is a great opportunity to reach families, both inside and outside the church, who find themselves in these situations. Teaching families healthier lifestyle habits is vitally important.

God has given parents the responsibility to teach their children proper health habits. The admonition in Proverbs 22:6 to train our children incorporates not only spiritual training but also lifestyle training. Teaching proper spiritual, physical, mental, and emotional balance is vital in raising children. If parents deal with stress by overeating, children will also. But if children see healthful foods placed in proper priority in the home, eating does not become the focus of their lives. If children see parents involved in an exercise program and experiencing fun family activities and if children are encouraged to participate in sports or other physical activities, these will become lifelong habits. Children learn through parental modeling.

> God has given parents the responsibility to teach their children proper health habits

A strong family-ministry program involves total fitness on a variety of levels. Offering one-evening seminars on nutrition or exercise can give families the basics to achieve a healthy, balanced lifestyle. Hospitals, health clubs, dietitians, and community health clinics are great places to seek resource persons to present this information. Ask church members to recommend resource persons in health and nutrition. A doctor or a nurse may know someone who would speak to your group on a volunteer basis. Be sure the persons you enlist are credible resources with strong experience and solid educational backgrounds who will share helpful information consistent with Christian teachings. As the coordinator for such an event, you have the responsibility to interview the presenters and to be aware of the material they will share. Be sure the topics covered will answer questions today's families face.

Offering such seminars before the Thanksgiving holiday, around the first of the new year, in the spring, or in the fall is usually successful. Seminars could be offered once a quarter or once a month to encourage continuing education. As an outreach tool, these seminars could be offered to the community.

An in-depth discipleship, nutrition/health-education, and accountability program that can help families is *Fit 4: A LifeWay Christian Wellness Plan* (see "Ministry Resources," beginning on p. 57). *Fit 4* is a biblically based and scripturally sound wellness plan that balances all areas of life: heart, soul, mind, and strength. The habits taught in *Fit 4* are taken home and incorporated into everyday life. When Mom begins to learn healthier alternatives to fast food, she presents better options for her family. When Dad learns to handle stress by turning to Christ instead of to ice cream, he sets a proper example for his children. Through the parents' example, children learn to take proper portions, read labels, and choose healthful snacks like fruits and vegetables.

Activity is also added to the family lifestyle. Instead of choosing to watch TV all evening, family members may walk or bicycle. Saturday events could include hikes, walking to and playing at the park, or helping an older couple plant a garden or wash the car. These activities require family members to be active, strong, and healthy.

To incorporate family activity into your church's family ministry, plan a Family

Olympics event at your church. Include activities for all ages from the youngest pre-schooler to the great-grandparent. Relay races, block-building contests, scavenger hunts, target games, and many other activities can be used to create a fun, lively event for everyone. Other ideas include a parent-child sports team and all-ages-welcome games of volleyball or softball. Use your imagination to create active events that get the family moving.

Christ's message to families can be shared in a variety of ways. You can make a difference in the spiritual and physical health of families in your church and community by providing seminars, studies, and fitness programs designed to build them up as families of God.

## Single-Parent Family Ministry

A church that wants to develop a ministry for single-parent families must take two preliminary steps. As with any other ministry the church undertakes, the first step must be prayer. The second component in developing this type of ministry is educating yourself and other leaders about single-parent families. Single-parent families come into the church at different stages of development, and they may experience several stages in their journey to become healthy, functioning families. Misunderstandings about this process can be detrimental not only to the church but also to the single-parent families your church is trying to reach.

> **A ministry to this group needs to include intervention and healing**

### Stages of Single Parenting

1. The first stage can be considered the crisis stage. These families are newly divorced or are experiencing the recent death of a parent. A ministry to this group needs to include intervention and healing through a grief- or divorce-recovery program for the parent and children. These families also have many needs that can encompass several other ministries of the church. This group may need financial assistance, help with parenting, and/or a support group.
2. The next stage of single parenting is the transitioning stage. Families are moving from crisis to the realization that though they have experienced a trauma, life goes forward. This stage also includes the transition from parenting with a partner to parenting alone. The parent needs classes or workshops on behavior and guidance. The parent also needs encouragement and perhaps financial assistance, help with budgeting, or other assistance.
3. In the third stage the single-parent family has experienced healing and is emerging as a healthy family. Parents in this group are ready to become involved with in-depth Bible studies. Many are so appreciative of God's grace that they are ready to serve the Lord with their talents, time, and finances.

### Developing a Ministry to Single-Parent Families

When your church has decided that it wants to develop a single-parent family ministry, follow these steps to get started.

1. It is important to start with a leadership team. Develop a core group of members who have an interest in single-parent families. This core group works best if it is composed of persons with a variety of interests and experiences. For example, you may want to include the following.
   - A single-parent mother
   - A single-parent father
   - A single adult who does not have children
   - A married couple that has a strong marriage and has been successful at parenting or a blended-family couple that has been married for several years and has

progressed through some of the stages involved in blending a family
- A representative from the church staff
- Representatives from single-adult ministry and family ministry
- Representatives from other ministries, such as women's, men's, care, children's, youth, and so on

**Seek God's guidance for the direction the ministry will take**

This group can meet, pray, and seek God's guidance for the direction the ministry will take and for who will be involved in developing the various components. Because single-parent family ministry encompasses so many other ministries of the church, all members of the core group need to be actively involved at the beginning. When the ministry is established, not all members need to continue with the ministry.

2. The next step is to develop a mission statement that coincides with the church's mission and family ministry's mission.

3. Begin your planning, remembering that single parents need relationships and mentoring, not programming. It will usually take several weeks to accomplish this step. Be sure to address these areas.
   - Leadership development
   - Child care and parenting issues
   - Financial needs
   - Counseling or support groups
   - Support for children
   - Outreach to the unchurched

4. Identify areas of concern for single parents.
   - Parenting, discipline, and setting boundaries
   - Legal and financial issues (housing, auto, child care)
   - Same-gender role models
   - Emotional and self-esteem
   - Friendships and relationships

5. Finally, set goals with time lines.

### Ways to Minister to Single Parents

Some churches may decide that they don't want to develop an extensive single-parent family ministry. If so, they can choose to minister to single parents with children.

1. If single parents are in a single-adult Bible study, set aside some time periodically to address parenting needs.

2. Hold a parenting workshop every quarter.

3. Include single-parent families in a parenting retreat with two-parent families.

4. When adult social functions or conferences are held, be sure to provide child care for children.

5. Conduct conferences on one or more of the following topics.
   - Biblical stewardship training
   - Communication skills
   - Healthy relationships
   - Spiritual growth through Bible study
   - Work skills and training

## Church Resources

As we have stated from the beginning, family ministry is not a base program like Bible teaching or discipleship training. Family ministry should permeate all the church does. It is unique in that it affects every aspect of church life and is dependent on every aspect of church life. For family ministry to be effective, it needs to tap the resources available in every arena of church life. "Evaluating and Assisting Church Programs to Minister to Family Members" on page 56 is a tool to help you assess where God is already working through ongoing church programs and where you need to join Him in ministering to the families in your church and community.

Examine the chart on page 56. First complete a copy of the chart by listing ministries and activities your church is already providing. Then go back and fill in a copy of the chart with ways your church can accomplish these ministries. Finally, complete the column "Need" based on the priorities you discovered through "Needs and Interests Survey" (see number 4, page 47). After listing the prioritized needs, meet with representatives of your church programs to evaluate the way the existing church programs can help meet these needs.

## Resources for Expanding Your Ministry to Families

### Local Associations

The purpose of local Southern Baptist associations of churches is to pool their collective resources to achieve a common goal. Whether that goal is feeding the hungry, ministering during local crises, or providing a community emphasis, the purpose is to help churches provide collectively what they cannot do as efficiently on their own. You may be affiliated with another association or alliance of churches in your community.

These associations or alliances can provide you with resources or can connect you with other churches to provide family opportunities for prevention, enrichment, intervention, and/or outreach. Many Baptist associations have a family-ministry director and committee who can provide training and assistance for developing your ministry to families.

**Associations pool their resources to achieve a common goal**

Contact your local association to discover what God may already be doing to minister to the needs of families in your church and community through other denominational ministries and community-assistance programs. Then you can discern how God wants you to join Him in filling the gaps. If you are unsure about whom to contact on the local level, ask your pastor or church-staff leader.

### State and Canadian Convention Resources

Another resource that is available to you and your family-ministry committee is your Baptist state convention, Canadian Baptist Convention, or district office. As associations have been formed to unite churches in ministry, state and Canadian conventions, districts, and dioceses have been formed to unite local associations of churches. Your convention's family-ministry director is there to provide you with training and assistance through your association. God has given you a multitude of resources to equip and support what God is doing through your church. The assistance each family-ministry director can offer may vary, but each has a heart for family ministry and will do all within his or her means to assist you.

Request assistance from your Baptist state convention's or Canadian Baptist Convention's family-ministry director. Convention offices are listed on page 63. When calling these numbers, ask for the state family-ministry director.

### LifeWay Christian Resources

LifeWay Christian Resources of the Southern Baptist Convention can also provide resources for developing your ministry to families. One obvious way is through printed resources, a list of which is provided on pages 57–59. These resources have been categorized according to target group (couples, parents, and so on), but they have also been marked according to the areas of ministry they can be used with (prevention, enrichment, intervention, and outreach).

You may also want to take advantage of the quality family magazines published by

# Evaluating and Assisting Church Programs to Minister to Family Members

| Need | Pastoral Ministry | Minister of Education | Deacon Ministry | Bible Teaching | Discipleship Training | Men's Ministry | Women's Ministry | Church Media Library | Prayer Ministry | Counseling Ministry |
|---|---|---|---|---|---|---|---|---|---|---|
| Comprehensive marriage ministry | Preach sermon series on covenant marriage. | Develop master plan for marriage ministry. | Become equipped to lead marriage-preparation sessions. | Provide Bible classes for engaged and married couples. | Provide groups on marriage preparation and enrichment. | Provide groups on what it means to be a Christlike husband. | Provide groups on what it means to be a godly wife. | Provide ongoing resources on covenant marriage. | Place engaged couples on the church's prayer list. | Set up schedule. Administer and interpret personality inventories. |
| | | | | | | | | | | |
| | | | | | | | | | | |
| | | | | | | | | | | |
| | | | | | | | | | | |

LifeWay. *HomeLife, BabyLife, ParentLife, Living with Teenagers, Journey, Stand Firm, Christian Single, Mature Living,* and *Christian Health* address specific issues within their targeted groups. Each magazine offers practical help for building strong families and addresses current social issues as well. However, one of the greatest benefits of these magazines is that they offer an opportunity to reach your community for Christ. Gaining entry to people's homes and capturing their attention are more difficult than ever. But a magazine gives your members something solid to share with a coworker, something substantial to leave door-to-door, or something extra to share with visitors.

Have you ever thought of using family magazines to support your church's family ministry? If not, consider ways you can use these magazines to their greatest potential. Don't let these valuable resources fall prey to mediocre methods of distribution, like being dumped on a table in an obscure corner of an assembly room or a hallway. Be a good steward of what God has entrusted to you in these valuable family magazines.

Chapter 2 mentioned that you can encourage families to reach out to the community by taking a prayer walk around the neighborhood. As families do this, they can also leave a copy of an appropriate magazine and a personal note from your church at each home. Then you can follow up with a contact and seek additional ministry opportunities with those families.

You may want to encourage families in your church to deliver an appropriate magazine along with a small gift to families who visit your church. Another way to use magazines in family ministry is to encourage families in your church to transform their homes into neighborhood evangelism centers, using magazines as a way of initiating meaningful contact with unsaved neighbors. You might want to have your pastor preach a sermon series on relational evangelism to launch this emphasis.

> **Deliver an appropriate magazine to families who visit your church**

Numerous opportunities exist to minister to families in your church and community through family magazines. As your family-ministry committee discovers where God is working in the church and community, take time to determine which of these magazines can help you meet the needs of particular families.

Another way LifeWay can assist you is by providing training in specific areas of ministry or in the general development of family ministry. This training is brought to you in several ways. One way is through the Baptist state or Canadian convention. These conventions periodically request that LifeWay provide leadership training in the area of family ministry. You may also ask your Baptist association to submit a request to the state convention for local leadership training conducted by LifeWay. Another way is through national leadership-training events. To receive more information about this training, call (615) 251-2275, see the Adult Discipleship and Family Web site at *www.lifeway.com/discipleplus*, or email *phil.waugh@lifeway.com*.

## Ministry Resources

The following key indicates the ministry areas addressed by the resources listed below.
◆ Prevention   ● Enrichment
✚ Intervention   ✳ Outreach

### Personal Growth
● *Experiencing God: Knowing and Doing the Will of God* by Henry Blackaby and Claude V. King
● *When God Speaks* by Henry Blackaby and Richard Blackaby
● *Experiencing God Bible*
● *In God's Presence: Your Daily Guide to a Meaningful Prayer Life* by T. W. Hunt and Claude V. King
● *Disciple's Prayer Life* by T. W. Hunt and Claude V. King

◆ ● *The Three Chairs: Experiencing Spiritual Breakthroughs* by Bruce Wilkinson

● *The Mind of Christ* by T. W. Hunt and Claude V. King

● *MasterLife* by Avery T. Willis Jr.

● *My Identity in Christ* by Gene Wilkes

◆ ● *Free to Forgive* by Robert Jeffress

✳ *Share Jesus Without Fear* by Bill Fay and Ralph Hodge

● *Choosing to Live the Blessing* by John Trent

● *The Vision of His Glory: Finding Hope Through the Revelation of Jesus Christ* by Anne Graham Lotz

◆ ● ✝ *How Now Shall We Live?* by Charles Colson and Nancy Pearcey

◆ ● *Truth Matters … for You and Tomorrow's Generation* by Josh McDowell

◆ ● ✳ *Fit 4: A LifeWay Christian Wellness Plan* by Branda Polk

◆ ● ✳ *Christian Health* magazine

◆ ● ✳ *Christian Single* magazine

◆ ● ✳ *Mature Living* magazine

● ✳ *Journey: A Woman's Guide to Intimacy with God* devotional magazine

● *A Woman's Heart: God's Dwelling Place* by Beth Moore

● *A Heart like His: Seeking the Heart of God Through a Study of David* by Beth Moore

● *To Live Is Christ: The Life and Ministry of Paul* by Beth Moore

● *Jesus, the One and Only* by Beth Moore

◆ ● ✝ ✳ *Breaking Free* by Beth Moore

● ✳ *In My Father's House: Women Relating to God as Father* by Mary Kassian

● *The Virtuous Woman: Shattering the Superwoman Myth* by Vicki Courtney

◆ ● *What Every Mom Needs* by Elisa Morgan and Carol Kuykendall

● *Life Lessons from Women in the Bible* by Rhonda Kelley

● ✳ *Stand Firm: God's Challenge for Today's Man* devotional magazine

● ✳ *The Seven Seasons of a Man's Life* by Patrick Morley

● ✳ *The Man God Uses* by Henry and Tom Blackaby

● *Men Leading the Charge* by Steve Farrar

## Marriage

◆ ● *Making Love Last Forever* by Gary Smalley

◆ ● *Covenant Marriage: Partnership and Commitment* by Diana Garland and Betty Hassler

◆ ● *Communication and Intimacy: Covenant Marriage* by Gary Chapman and Betty Hassler

◆ ● ✳ *The Five Love Languages* by Gary Chapman

● *Building Relationships: A Discipleship Guide for Married Couples* by Gary Chapman

◆ ✳ *Counsel for the Nearly and Newly Married* by Ernest White and James E. White

● *I Take Thee to Be My Spouse: Bible Study for Newlyweds*, edited by David Apple

● *Experiencing God as Couples* by Henry and Marilynn Blackaby

◆ ● ✳ *Money in Marriage* by Larry Burkett

## ● ✳ Marriage Training-and-Enrichment Events

Call (800) 254-2022 for a current schedule of marriage training-and-enrichment events in your area or visit *www.lifeway.com/discipleplus.*

## Parenting

◆ ● *Empowered Parenting* by Robert J. Morgan

◆ ● *Grandparenting by Grace* by Irene M. Endicott and C. Ferris Jordan

◆ ● *Parenting by Grace: Discipline and Spiritual Growth* by Dixie Ruth Crase and Arthur H. Criscoe

◆ ● *Shaping the Next Generation* by David and Elaine Atchison

- ◆ ● *The Five Love Languages of Children* by Gary Chapman
- ◆ ● *ParentProject: Tools for Godly Parenting* by William and Martha Sears
- ● *Choosing to Live the Blessing* by John Trent
- ● *The Three Chairs: Experiencing Spiritual Breakthroughs* by Bruce Wilkinson
- ● ✷ *BabyLife* magazine
- ● ✷ *ParentLife* magazine
- ● ✷ *Living with Teenagers* magazine

## Families

- ◆ ● ✷ *Choice Creations* tracts
- ◆ ● *Building Strong Families* by William Mitchell
- ◆ ● *Peace in the Family: A Home Activity Book* by William Mitchell and Mikey Oldham
- ◆ ● *Self-Control in the Family: A Home Activity Book* by William Mitchell and Phyllis Belew
- ◆ ● *Kindness in the Family: A Home Activity Book* by William Mitchell and Wanda King
- ◆ ● *Prayer in the Family: A Home Activity Book* by William Mitchell and Cindy Pitts
- ◆ ● *Truth Matters … for You and Tomorrow's Generation* by Josh McDowell
- ◆ ● *Right from Wrong—What You Need to Know to Help Youth Make Right Choices* by Josh McDowell and Bob Hostleter
- ◆ ● ✚ ✷ *New Faces in the Frame: A Guide to Marriage and Parenting in the Blended Family* by Dick Dunn
- ● ✷ *Family to Family* by Jerry Pipes and Victor Lee
- ● *Choosing to Live the Blessing* by John Trent
- ◆ ● *The Three Chairs: Experiencing Spiritual Breakthroughs* by Bruce Wilkinson
- ● ✷ *HomeLife* magazine

### ● Family Training-and-Enrichment Events

Call (800) 254-2022 for a current schedule of family training-and-enrichment events in your area or visit *www.lifeway.com/discipleplus*.

## Support Groups

- ✚ ✷ *WiseCounsel: Skills for Lay Counseling* by John W. Drakeford and Claude V. King
- ✚ ✷ *LIFE Support Group Series* Training Video
- ✚ ✷ *Untangling Relationships: A Christian Perspective on Codependency* by Pat Springle
- ✚ ✷ *Making Peace with Your Past* by Tim Sledge
- ✚ ✷ *Moving Beyond Your Past* by Tim Sledge
- ✚ ✷ *Search for Significance: LIFE Support Edition* by Robert S. McGee
- ✚ ✷ *Breaking the Cycle of Hurtful Family Experiences* by Robert S. McGee, Pat Springle, Jim Craddock, and Dale McCleskey
- ✚ ✷ *Shelter from the Storm: Hope for Survivors of Sexual Abuse* by Cynthia Kubetin, James Mallory, and Jacque Truitt
- ✚ ✷ *A Time for Healing: Coming to Terms with Your Divorce* by Harold Ivan Smith
- ✚ ✷ *Recovering from the Losses of Life: LIFE Support Series Edition* by H. Norman Wright
- ✚ ✷ *Faithful and True: Sexual Integrity in a Fallen World* by Mark R. Laaser and Eldridge Machen

For more information about these and other resources, write to LifeWay Church Resources Customer Service; 127 Ninth Avenue, North; Nashville, TN 37234-0113; fax (615) 251-5933; call toll free 1-800-458-2772; email *customerservice@lifeway.com*; order online at *www.lifeway.com*; or visit a LifeWay Christian Store. For more information on training opportunities, call (615) 251-2275. For more information on enrichment events, call (800) 254-2022.

## Other Churches

Often, other churches in the community provide shared ministries to families. Usually, these are crisis-intervention ministries, such as food pantries, clothing closets, emergency funds, counseling, and so forth. Look for ministries in which God is working and be willing to join Him in the ministries that are addressed by your mission statement.

One opportunity to involve other churches and the community is the Building Strong Families campaign. This program and supporting study materials effectively teach families through churches and schools how to make their homes training centers for building moral character. For additional information on how your church and association can become a catalyst for joining God in this ministry, contact Phil Waugh at LifeWay by calling (615) 251-2275 or *email phil.waugh@lifeway.com.*

## Community Resources

The final group of tools to meet families' needs is community resources. Because many of these resources are secular, you must determine whether God wants you to become involved in them. When Jesus instructs us to minister to the poor and the oppressed, He speaks directly to the church, not to the government agencies of His day or our day. We have a responsibility to minister to the needs of families and to influence our government agencies through our actions. Separation of church and state may be the clarion call of our day, but the church needs to lead the state by its example.

Use the following chart to determine where God wants your church to join Him in ministering to families.

# Community Resources for Meeting Needs

| Needs of Your Church/ Community | Helpful Resources | | | | | Gaps Your Church Can Fill |
|---|---|---|---|---|---|---|
| Money management | Bankers | Investment/ financial services | Local colleges | Libraries | County extension | |
| Parent-child relationship | Counselors | School system | Children's homes | Big Brother program | Child-care centers | |
| Unemployment | Chamber of Commerce | Employment agencies | Referral services | Local merchants | Family services | |
| Teen suicide prevention | Psychologists/ counselors | 24-hour crisis centers | Mental-health centers | Juvenile centers | Hospitals | |

[1]To calculate your Body Mass Index, go to *www.fit4.com* and look under the heading "Strength."
[2]Michael Fumento, "Why We Need a New War on Weight," *USA Weekend*, 14–17 September 1997, 4.
[3]Ibid.
[4]Richard B. Parr, "Exercising to Lose 10 to 20 Pounds," *The Physician and Sportsmedicine*, April 1997, <*http://www.physsportsmed.com/issues/1997/04apr/lose.htm*> (12 November 1997).

# The Promotion of Family Ministry

# Chapter 9

Wouldn't you like to involve every member of your church in some aspect of family ministry? Getting everyone involved is a commendable goal but not a realistic one for most churches. In a perfect world everyone would understand the importance of establishing a healthy family and would be eager to participate in all activities that build strong families. The reality is that some people feel no need to grow in their family relationships. Effective promotion, however, can target, inform, motivate, and involve those who are open to participation in family-growth opportunities.

## Understanding Your Audience

Churches are composed primarily of three kinds of people: the die-hards, the drop-ins, and the do-littles. Some of these are very reachable for family-ministry activities, while

others are not. This doesn't mean that you should write off the unreachables; it just means that you should be realistic about getting everyone involved in family-ministry activities. You have probably already begun to think of persons in your church who qualify as die-hards, drop-ins, or do-littles. The purpose of these categories is not to judge others but to understand the challenge of providing programs and activities that meet their particular family needs.

> **Be realistic about getting everyone involved**

## Promoting Family Ministry

Let's explore ways you can reach people for family-ministry programs and events. You must definitely promote family ministry among all people you want to reach. If you have already decided that your efforts are best directed at the die-hards and drop-ins, you are probably correct. After all, they are most likely to participate in what you offer. The surest way to make family ministry visible is to provide a high-quality ministry that meets the needs of families in the church and community. Nothing inspires confidence more than a reputation for excellence. Satisfied "customers" do more for family ministry than all the promotion you can plan.

### The Four Cs of Effective Promotion

People have more options for using their time than ever before. To compete successfully with the other activities, you must give people sufficient reasons to participate in family-ministry experiences. Effective promotion passes the test of the four Cs: it must capture people's attention, communicate value, convince people to participate, and confront them repeatedly with a message. Ask these questions about your publicity.

1. Does it *capture* people's attention? Does it make them want to listen or read further?
2. Does it *communicate* value? Do people understand how their lives will be enriched and how they will benefit from the experience?
3. Does it *convince* people to participate? Are they moved to action, to make a commitment to participate? Is the message strong enough to make them set aside the time to be involved?
4. Does it continually *confront* the target audience with the message? What different media are you using to deliver the message?

## Choose the Best Promotional Methods

The best avenues through which to promote family-ministry activities to church members are corporate worship, Bible study, and discipleship training. A number of methods can be used to publicize family-ministry programs and activities inside and outside the church.

- Verbal and written announcements
- Newsletters and brochures
- Catalogs
- Letters and cards
- Personal encouragement
- Posters and displays in heavy-traffic areas
- Family magazines in high-traffic areas
- Promotional place mats at Wednesday-evening meals or at churchwide fellowships
- Skits in worship services and in Bible-study departments and classes
- Discounts for early registration if a fee is charged
- Displays in the church media library
- Sermon series related to families
- Distribution of registration forms at exits following services
- Registration tables at key entrances prior to the activity
- Telephone teams to make calls
- Notes sent home in diaper bags
- Notes sent home through Mother's Day Out and after-school programs
- Family-focused fellowship following a special event
- Web site

> **High-quality promotional materials are within the reach of almost any church**

One church produces an annual catalog describing all family studies, programs, events, and activities it will offer during the coming year. This catalog is sent to all church members and is made available for families to distribute in the community. Though many churches may not be able to afford such a catalog, every church can provide an information sheet that describes the family activities that will be provided during the coming year. Due to the availability of low-cost computer technology, high-quality promotional materials are within the reach of almost any church today.

Desktop publishing programs make promotion easy. You don't have to be a computer genius to produce great-looking brochures, newsletters, and posters. A number of companies provide religious clip art on disks that can be imported into your publications. Among these are LifeWay's clip-art packet and clip-art disks.[1]

Your church can make available to the public family-enrichment events such as marriage-enrichment retreats or parenting seminars. Invite the community to participate with no strings attached. Buy space in the print media and time on local radio and television stations to promote these events. Make sure that your promotion is of high quality. Let the news media know what is being done. Encourage members to let their friends know and to participate in these activities.

The greatest promotion of all comes in the form of changed lives, changed families, and a changed church. When a church allows God's presence and activity to be expressed through individuals, marriages, and families, a watching world will be drawn to Him. The greatest form of promotion comes through excited, involved people. It is imperative that families in your church and community see the commitment and catch the excitement for family ministry.

---

[1]Order from LifeWay Church Resources Customer Service; 127 Ninth Avenue, North; Nashville, TN 37234-0113; fax (615) 251-5933; email *customerservice@lifeway.com;* visit *www.lifeway.com;* call toll free (800) 458-2772; or visit a LifeWay Christian Store.

# State Convention Family-Ministry Offices

Alabama Baptist State Convention
P. O. Box 11870
Montgomery, AL 36111-0870
Phone: (800) 264-1225

Alaska Baptist Convention
1750 O'Malley Road
Anchorage, AK 99516
Phone: (907) 344-9627

Arizona Southern Baptist Convention
4520 North Central Avenue, Suite 560
Phoenix, AZ 85012-1835
Phone (602) 240-3280

Arkansas Baptist State Convention
525 West Capitol
Little Rock, AR 72201-3309
Phone: (501) 376-4791

California Southern Baptist Convention
678 East Shaw Avenue
Fresno, CA 93710
Phone: (559) 229-9533

Canadian Convention of Southern
Baptists
100 Convention Way
Cochrane, Alberta, Canada T4C 262
Phone: (403) 932-5688

Colorado Baptist General Convention
7393 South Alton Way
Englewood, CO 80112-2372
Phone: (303) 771-6272

Dakota Southern Baptist Fellowship
2020 Lovett
Bismarck, ND 58504-6737
Phone: (701) 255-3765

District of Columbia Baptist Convention
1628 Sixteenth Street, NW
Washington, DC 20009-3099
Phone: (202) 667-8258

Florida Baptist Convention
1230 Hendricks Avenue
Jacksonville, FL 32207-8696
Phone: (904) 396-2351

Georgia Baptist Convention
2930 Flowers Road, South
Atlanta, GA 30341-5562
Phone: (770) 455-0404

Hawaii Pacific Baptist Convention
2042 Vancouver Drive
Honolulu, HI 96822-2491
Phone: (808) 946-9581

Illinois Baptist State Association
3085 Stevenson Drive
Springfield, IL 62703-4440
Phone: (217) 786-2600

State Convention of Baptists in Indiana
900 North High School Road
Indianapolis, IN 46214-3759
Phone: (317) 241-9317

Baptist Convention of Iowa
2400 86th Street, Suite 27
Des Moines, IA 50322-4331
Phone: (515) 278-1566

Kansas/Nebraska Convention of
Southern Baptists
5410 SW Seventh Street
Topeka, KS 66606-2398
Phone: (785) 273-4880

Kentucky Baptist Convention
10701 Shelbyville Road
Louisville, KY 40243-0433
Phone: (502) 245-4101

Louisiana Baptist Convention
1250 MacArthur Drive
Alexandria, LA 71309
Phone: (318) 448-3402

Baptist Convention of Maryland/Delaware
10255 Old Columbia Road
Columbia, MD 21046-1736
Phone: (410) 290-5290

Baptist State Convention of Michigan
15635 West Twelve Mile Road
Southfield, MI 48076-3091
Phone: (248) 557-4200

Minnesota/Wisconsin Southern Baptist
Convention
519 16th Street, SE
Rochester, MN 55904-5296
Phone: (507) 282-3636

Mississippi Baptist Convention Board
515 Mississippi Street
Jackson, MS 39201-1702
Phone: (601) 968-3800

Missouri Baptist Convention
400 East High Street
Jefferson City, MO 65101-3215
Information: (800) 736-6227
Phone: (573) 635-7931

Montana Southern Baptist Fellowship
1130 Cerise Road
Billings, MT 59101
Phone: (406) 252-7537

Nevada Baptist Convention
406 California Avenue
Reno, NV 89509-1520
Phone: (702) 786-0406

Baptist Convention of New England
87 Lincoln
Northborough, MA 01532-1742
Phone: (508) 393-6013

Baptist Convention of New Mexico
616 Central Avenue, SE
Albuquerque, NM 87103
Phone: (505) 247-0586

Baptist Convention of New York
6538 Old Collamer Road
East Syracuse, NY 13057-1013
Phone: (315) 433-1001

Baptist State Convention of North
Carolina
205 Convention Drive
Cary, NC 27511
Phone: (919) 467-5100

Northwest Baptist Convention
3200 NE, 109th Avenue
Vancouver, WA 98682-7749
Phone: (360) 882-2100

State Convention of Baptists in Ohio
1680 East Broad Street
Columbus, OH 43203-2095
Phone: (614) 258-8491

Baptist General Convention of Oklahoma
3800 North May Avenue
Oklahoma City, OK 73112-6506
Phone: (405) 942-3000

Baptist Convention of Pennsylvania/
South Jersey
4620 Fritchey Street
Harrisburg, PA 17109-2895
Phone: (717) 652-5856

South Carolina Baptist Convention
190 Stoneridge Drive
Columbia, SC 29210-8239
Phone: (803) 765-0030

Tennessee Baptist Convention
5001 Maryland Way
Brentwood, TN 37027
Phone: (615) 373-2255

Baptist General Convention of Texas
333 North Washington
Dallas, TX 75246-1798
Phone: (214) 828-5100

Utah/Idaho Southern Baptist
Convention
12401 South GI 450 East
Draper, UT 84020-1347
Phone: (801) 572-5350

Virginia Baptist Resource Center
2828 Emerywood Parkway
Richmond, VA 23294
Phone: (804) 672-2100

West Virginia Convention of Southern
Baptists
Number One Mission Way
Scott Depot, WV 25560-9406
Phone: (304) 757-0944

Wyoming Southern Baptist Convention
3925 Casper Mountain Road
Casper, WY 82601
Phone: (307) 472-4087

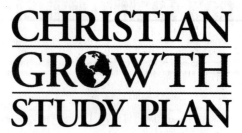

# CHRISTIAN GROWTH STUDY PLAN

*Preparing Christians to Serve*

In the **Christian Growth Study Plan (formerly the Church Study Course)** this book, *How to Minister to Families in Your Church,* is a resource for course credit. To receive credit, read the book; complete the learning activities; show your work to your pastor, a staff member, or a church leader; then complete the following information. This page may be duplicated. Send the completed page to:

Christian Growth Study Plan, MSN 117
127 Ninth Avenue, North
Nashville, TN 37234-0117
Fax: (615) 251-5067

For information about the Christian Growth Study Plan, refer to the current *Christian Growth Study Plan Catalog.* Your church office may have a copy. If not, request a free copy from the Christian Growth Study Plan office, (615) 251-2525.

## How to Minister to Families in Your Church
## COURSE NUMBER: LS-0034 (Family Enrichment)
### PARTICIPANT INFORMATION

### PARTICIPANT INFORMATION

| Social Security Number (USA ONLY) | Personal CGSP Number* | Date of Birth (MONTH, DAY, YEAR) |
|---|---|---|
| Name (First, Middle, Last) | Home Phone | |
| Address (Street, Route, or P.O. Box) | City, State, or Province | Zip/Postal Code |

### CHURCH INFORMATION

| Church Name | | |
|---|---|---|
| Address (Street, Route, or P.O. Box) | City, State, or Province | Zip/Postal Code |

### CHANGE REQUEST ONLY

| ☐ Former Name | | |
|---|---|---|
| ☐ Former Address | City, State, or Province | Zip/Postal Code |
| ☐ Former Church | City, State, or Province | Zip/Postal Code |

| Signature of Pastor, Conference Leader, or Other Church Leader | Date |
|---|---|

*New participants are requested but not required to give SS# and date of birth.  Existing participants, please give CGSP# when using SS# for the first time. Thereafter, only one ID# is required.  **Mail to:** Christian Growth Study Plan, 127 Ninth Ave., North, Nashville, TN 37234-0117. Fax: (615)251-5067

Rev. 6-99